OSPREY COMBAT AIRCRAFT • 32

B-25
MITCHELL UNITS
OF THE MTO

SERIES EDITOR: TONY HOLMES

OSPREY COMBAT AIRCRAFT • 32

B-25 MITCHELL UNITS OF THE MTO

Steve Pace

OSPREY
PUBLISHING

Front Cover
B-25J-10s 43-27784 and 43-27800 (nicknamed *BOTTOMS-UP II*) of the 486th BS/340th BG depart their base at Alesan Field, on the island of Corsica, on the afternoon of 20 February 1945 and head for axis targets in and around the Po River Valley in northern Italy. Once aloft, the bombers took their place in a six-aeroplane box along with four other B-25s, before joining up with two similar sized boxes in a staggered formation. Three additional Mitchells – called the chaff element – also took their place alongside the 18 lead aircraft. The previous '6V' (43-4082 *BOTTOMS-UP*), piloted by Lt James Voelkers, had crashed mysteriously minutes after take-off on 18 March 1944. None of its crewmembers were ever found, although the wreckage of the B-25 was discovered several weeks later in the mountains of northern Corsica (*Cover artwork by Iain Wyllie*)

For a catalogue of all Osprey Publishing titles please contact us at:

Osprey Direct UK, PO Box 140, Wellingborough, Northants NN8 4ZA, UK
E-mail: info@ospreydirect.co.uk

Osprey Direct USA, c/o Motorbooks International, 729 Prospect Ave, PO Box 1, Osceola, WI 54020, USA
E-mail: info@ospreydirectusa.com

Or visit our website:
www.ospreypublishing.com

First published in Great Britain in 2002 by Osprey Publishing
Elms Court, Chapel Way, Botley, Oxford, OX2 9LP

ISBN 1 84176 284 9

Edited by Tony Holmes
Page design by Tony Truscott
Cover Artwork by Iain Wyllie
Aircraft Profiles by Jim Laurier
Scale Drawings by Mark Styling
Origination by Grasmere Digital Imaging, Leeds, UK
Printed through Bookbuilders, Hong Kong

02 03 04 05 06 10 9 8 7 6 5 4 3 2 1

ACKNOWLEDGEMENTS
I wish to thank the following individuals – NCO Robert E 'Bob' Wilson, Group Intelligence, HQ 12th BG (M); David Ward; Mike Laney for his Grandfather, 1Lt William P Laney, Pilot, 486th BS (M); V Robert Haney; S/Sgt Dana H Craig, Top Turret Gunner, 486th BS (M); Amy Murphy Demeo for her Father, S/Sgt Brendon J Murphy, Top Turret Gunner, 445th BS (M); Sally Heim; Katherine Williams, Museum of Flight; Henry J Del Percio; Erich Hetzel for his Father, T/Sgt Thomas A Hetzel, Radioman, 487th BS (M); Norman E Taylor; Bert Kinzey, Detail & Scale Copyright Drawings by Lloyd S Jones; Dave Mershon, 487th BS (M); Ray Ostlie, 380th BS (M); Fred Pierce; S/Sgt George Underwood, T/Sgt Ben Guild, Radio Operator/Gunner, 447th BS (M); Top Turret Gunner, 381st BS (M); 2/Lt Kenneth L Voight, Navigator, 82nd BS (M); Guy Julien, contributor to the 57th BW Research List; 1Lt Bill Poole, Pilot, 379th BS (M); Chris Wamsley; Dave McLaren; Capt Richard E Krause, Bombardier, 445th BS (M); O James Hicks for his Father, S/Sgt George G Hicks, Tail Gunner and Gunnery Instructor, 83rd BS (M); Don Kaiser; T/Sgt John Jarvis, Radioman, 445th BS (M); Stan Piet; Tom Britton; Confederate Air Force; John Bodinhammer; Paul Bill, Museum of Aviation; S/Sgt Peter A Law, Historian, 12th FTW/HO; Rob Dubois; Fred Hayner, 'Hayner the Painter'; John P Kelley; 1Lt Ed Crinnion, Pilot, 446th BS (M); Harry D George Jr for his Father, Harry D George, and the men of the 487th BS (M); Capt Glenn T Black, Pilot, 381st BS (M); Jack Cook; Bob Silliman; Quentin Kaiser; Paul Gale; T/Sgt Isidore Ifshin, Engineer/Top Turret Gunner, 447th BS (M); Versolato Giuseppe; 2/Lt Victor Ramirez, Pilot, 488th BS (M) and his son Michael; Mark Adamic; Group Editors Alex Adair (12th BG), Charles Brewton, Esther Oyster (310th BG), George Mercca, Paul Peck (321th BG); Leonard Kauffmann and Nick Loveless (340th BG); and finally the volume *The B-25 Over the Med - the 50th Anniversary*, published by the 57th BW Association in 1992.

CONTENTS

INTRODUCTION

William 'Billy' Mitchell was one of America's staunchest supporters of air power, and he fought relentlessly for its establishment throughout his tenure of military service. So intense was his fight that it ultimately cost him his career as vice commander of the US Army Air Service (USAAS). Subsequent to his actions, he was erroneously court-martialled in 1925 for his beliefs, and reduced in rank from brigadier-general to colonel. Mitchell was also reassigned to a desk job. This fiasco came after he had actually proved in 1921 that USAAS bombers like the Martin MB-2 could indeed sink armoured battleships.

However, by the time of Mitchell's untimely death in 1936 at the age of 57, the US military establishment had come to realise just how wrong it had been, and more importantly, just how right he had been all along. Posthumously then, 'Billy' Mitchell was promoted to the rank of major-general, and he is widely acknowledged today as one of the most respected founders of US air power.

North American Aviation (NAA) did not want to leave 'Billy' Mitchell's good name fading away on some dreary headstone in an obscure graveyard, and shortly after its prototype B-25 medium bomber appeared in 1940, in an official naming ceremony with his sister Ruth in attendance, the new twin-engined bomber was appropriately named Mitchell. On the left bomb-bay door, his sister boldly inscribed in chalk, 'For "Fighting Billy". His Bomber', signed Ruth.

As it happened, one of Mitchell's staunchest advocates, NAA's Lee Atwood, stated, 'Very early in the (B-25) project several of us were having a bull session in "Dutch" Kindleberger's office and the subject of a name for the new bomber was brought up. I suggested that it should be named after Gen "Billy" Mitchell but nothing was decided at that time. In a later conversation we settled on Mitchell.'

When in fact the B-25 was officially named Mitchell, in essence, 'Billy' Mitchell had been reborn.

The B-25 more than lived up to its namesake during World War 2, helping in a big way to prove the true value of air power. More than 10,500 Mitchells were built, some 9800 for the US Army Air Corps-cum-US Army Air Forces alone. In every combat zone – not just the Mediterranean Theatre of Operations (MTO) – the B-25s, and the men who manned and maintained them, let it be known that 'Billy' Mitchell had indeed been correct about his beliefs in future confrontations. That is, his ideas on air power were truly to be the way of future warfare.

During the course of the campaign in the MTO, the five medium bomb groups, and their 20 squadrons, used their respective allotments of B-25s to their fullest potential. From low-altitude strafing missions to high-altitude bombing sorties, the Mitchells of the Ninth and Twelfth Air Forces proved themselves to be a very successful brood of combat aircraft.

The B-25 was already a famed medium bomber by the time it started arriving in the MTO in mid-1942, for on 18 April that same year, Lt Col James H 'Jimmy' Doolittle had led 16 B-25Bs from the deck of the USS *Hornet* on the now legendary attack on Japan.

The Mitchell's vital statistics were as follows – powered by two Wright R-2600 Cyclone engines, the bomber, in its final configuration (the B-25J), was 53 ft 5.75 in long, had a wingspan of 67 ft 6.7 in and a height of 16 ft 6.19 in. Its maximum combat take-off weight was 33,400 lbs (the J-model could carry a bomb load of up to 4000 lb) and its maximum speed was 293 mph at 13,850 ft. In combat configuration, the aircraft was typically crewed by a pilot, co-pilot, navigator, bombardier and two gunners.

The five B-25 bomb groups of the Ninth and Twelfth Air Forces, and the 57th BW, were the 12th BG (Medium), 310th BG (M), 319th BG (M), 321st BG (M) and 340th BG (M). Each controlled four squadrons, and these were assigned a maximum of 25 aircraft apiece. During three full years of combat operations – mid 1942 to mid 1945 – these groups used five different models of Mitchell, namely the B-25C, D. G, H and J. Considering that these 20 squadrons each employed as many as five different models of B-25 during the three-year campaign in the Mediterranean, at least 2000 Mitchells saw action in the

MTO between 1942 and 1945.

NINTH AND TWELFTH AIR FORCES

Whether daytime or night-time, the Mitchell units in the MTO bombed and strafed all sorts of targets that included airfields, artillery positions and anti-aircraft artillery (AAA) batteries, barracks, bridges, canals, convoys, command, control and communications centres, factories, hangars, railway lines, roads, ships, shipyards, tanks, trains and rolling stock, troops, trucks and anything else being exploited and/or operated by the Axis powers. These B-25s were operated by both the Ninth and Twelfth Air Forces.

The emergence of what was to become the Ninth Air Force in the MTO came about in June 1942 when a detachment of B-24 Liberators landed in Egypt. Under the command of Col Harry Halverson, 13 of these bombers carried out the first raid on the oil fields at Ploesti, in Romania, during Operation *Tidal Wave*. With orders to consolidate several aircraft units in Egypt into the Middle East Air Force (MEAF), Maj Gen Lewis H Brereton took command on 28 June 1942. Five months later, on 12 November, MEAF became the Ninth Air Force, still under the command of Gen Brereton.

Between November 1942 and September 1943 the Ninth Air Force supported the Allied North African campaign that defeated Rommel's *Afrika Korps*, then provided air support for the invasions of Sicily and Italy. By 31 January 1943, Ninth Air Force units had flown 6023 sorties, dropped 3811 tons of bombs, claimed 77 enemy aircraft destroyed (with another 67 probable or damaged) and lost 47 of its own aircraft.

During 22-24 August 1943, after conducting many additional strikes against Ploesti, and targets in Sicily, Italy and southern Austria, the Ninth Air Force transferred its medium bomber units to the Twelfth Air Force and moved to England.

The origins of the Twelfth Air Force can be traced back to a series of meetings that were conducted in mid 1942 when the Allied Powers' planners were developing a strategy for the invasion of North Africa, codenamed Operation *Torch*. Because this extensive operation would require a new organisation to provide enough manpower and equipment to support it, plans for the activation of the Twelfth Air Force were prepared simultaneously with the invasion strategy.

On 20 August 1942, the Twelfth Air Force was activated at Bolling Field, in Washington DC. On 23 September, Brig Gen James H 'Jimmy' Doolittle formally assumed command of the Twelfth Air

The 12th BG was the first medium bomb group to be based in North Africa, arriving in-theatre in August 1942. This particular B-25C-1 (41-13123) was assigned to the 82nd BS and named *OLD WAR HOSS* (*NASM via Bob Haney*)

Two early-build B-25Cs from the 81st BS/12th BG head out on yet another mission over featureless Tunisian desert in late 1942. After its successful participation in the North African campaign, the group saw further action during the invasion of both Sicily and Italy, before being reassigned to the Tenth Air Force in the China-Burma-India (CBI) theatre. The 12th BG arrived in India on 21 March 1944, and flew its first CBI mission on 16 April (*USAF*)

Force, and he chose Col Hoyt S Vandenberg to be his chief of staff – Lt Col Roger J Browne (26-28 August 1942) and Lt Col Harold L Neely (28 August to 23 September 1942) had preceded him, both of whom had served on a temporary basis. Doolittle, who planned and led the famed raid on Japan some five months earlier, proved to be an excellent commander.

Lt Gen Carl A 'Tooey' Spaatz replaced Gen Doolittle as commander of the Twelfth on 1 March 1943, and he was followed by Lt Gen John K Cannon on 21 December 1943, Maj Gen Benjamin W Chidlaw on 2 April 1945 and Brig Gen Charles T Myers on 26 May 1945.

Barely three months after it had been conceived, the Twelfth Air Force made its first contribution to World War 2. When the day arrived for the invasion of North Africa, on 8 November 1942, the Twelfth was ready to meet its obligations.

By 18 February 1943, when the Twelfth Air Force merged with Royal Air Force units to form the Northwest African Air Forces (NAAF) in the first assembling of various allied air forces under one command, the Twelfth's strength had grown to 1038 aeroplanes. Lt Gen Spaatz, who had been instrumental in the formation of the Twelfth, was then placed in command of NAAF. As the days lengthened and spring arrived, Spaatz's forces proceeded with the arduous and necessary task of whittling down the Luftwaffe in Tunisia.

A constant problem facing the Allies in those days was how to find enough fighters to protect the bombers from the still very real threat posed by German and Italian fighters. Having suffered losses at the hands of Axis fighters during poorly escorted daylight raids at medium altitude in late 1942, the Liberator-equipped 97th BG had been joined in early December by three squadrons of B-24s from the 92nd BG. These aircraft were to undertake strategic bombing from high altitude, and as production allowed, B-25s and B-26s were rushed to the MTO to take over tactical bombing duties from the vulnerable B-24s.

Aircraft '33' (B-25C 41-12863) was assigned to Capt Doug Spawn and his crew when this photograph was taken on 9 January 1943. Part of the 12th BG's 82nd BS, the aircraft is seen in a mixed formation with other 12th BG B-25s and Baltimore IIIs from the RAF's No 232 Wing. The aircraft were heading for the axis-held Mareth Line, in Tunisia. Note the solitary P-40K from the 57th FG providing fighter escort immediately above Spawn's Mitchell (*via 12th BG Association*)

The Allies experienced numerous setbacks during the Tunisian campaign. For example, when Gen Erwin Rommel drove his Panzers through the Kasserine Pass on 20 February 1943, everything with wings was thrown against him, including the heavy bombers flying below medium altitude (8000 to 10,000 ft). But there were also 'red-letter' days like the famous 18 April 1943 'Palm Sunday Massacre', when P-40s of the 57th FG caught a large formation of Ju 52/3ms and Me 323s flying men and supplies to Rommel's forces, and duly shot down 76 aircraft in a victory reminiscent of the Battle of Britain.

NAAF's first great achievement was the establishment of complete air superiority over North Africa. The second was the interdiction of

B-25C-1 41-13078 *WOLF PACK* of the 380th BS/310th BG has its load of six 500-lb general-purpose bombs prepared by an armourer prior to them being winched into the bomb-bay in late 1942. The 380th and 381st BSs were the first medium bomb groups to use the then 'hush-hush' Norden bombsight in the MTO, these being installed in their new 41-13XXX series B-25C-1s (*M McCandlish via Bob Haney*)

supply lines to Tunisia by bombing ports, sinking ships and downing vulnerable aerial convoys, which were the enemy's last resort.

The third contribution of the Twelfth Air Force to the great victory was the intense close support of ground troops in the final breakthrough. Mounting concentrations of Allied aircraft were utilised for the March 1943 offensive that broke through the Mareth Line, and for the final assaults on Tunis and Bizerta.

With the final collapse – after 191 days – of the Axis forces in North Africa on 18 May 1943, the Twelfth was free to turn its attention across the Mediterranean Sea to what Winston Churchill once called the 'soft underbelly' of *Festung Europe* (Fortress Europe). During the course of the North African campaign, Allied air forces had dropped 11,708 tons of bombs, downed 1304 aircraft and sunk 76 ships. American and British aircraft losses totalled 651.

The striking power amassed for this campaign was now used to reduce axis resistance on the 32-square-mile Italian island of Pantelleria, which surrendered on 11 June 1943 with 10,000 prisoners after 12 days of relentless attacks by aircraft of the Ninth and Twelfth Air Forces. This was history's first example of territorial conquest by air action alone, and it proved to be a great victory – and a relatively inexpensive one. Losing 63 aircraft, the Allies claimed 236 enemy machines in return, and gained fighter bases that would prove to be indispensable for the invasion of Sicily.

The next mission for the Twelfth Air Force, and its British co-partner in NAAF, was the destruction of Axis air power on Sicily. Between 1 July and the Sicilian D-Day on 10 July, 3000 sorties were flown against airfields both on the island and the Italian mainland.

After Sicily, inevitably, came Italy. On 9 September the US Fifth Army, together with British and Canadian forces, landed on the Italian mainland south of Naples at Salerno. During the previous weeks the heavy and medium bombers of the Twelfth had softened up the enemy for the attack. They destroyed airfields, thus keeping aircraft on the ground, and their escorts had weakened the striking power of the Luftwaffe by decimating its fighter formations, which had risen to meet them. The first objective during the invasion of Italy was to disrupt the enemy's flow of supplies and reinforcements, and to isolate German divisions by devastating communication and railroad systems.

To this end, Italy was raked from its 'boot toe' to the Brenner Pass, in the Alps, with NAAF flying 4419 sorties and dropping 6230 tons of bombs between 17 August and 6 September.

Taking the Italian D-Day as an example of what the Twelfth could achieve in combat, it committed its full offensive force to securing the beachhead by effectively isolating Salerno from Axis reinforcements. Between 9-11 September, its aeroplanes flew 1006 sorties and dropped 1679 tons of bombs,

Truly a combat veteran, B-25J *The Early Bird III* saw much action with the 487th BS/340th BG in 1943. Thankfully, the significance of its nose-art remains a mystery! *The Early Bird III* survived rather longer in the frontline than the group's original CO, Col Mills, who was shot down and killed over Furney, in Algeria, on 6 May 1943 while leading one of the group's early missions (*Harry D George Jr Collection*)

achieving virtually complete interruption of motor vehicles and trains on the main road and rail links that led to the region. Finally, the spectacular strafing of some 200 Ju 88s at Foggia allowed the beachhead to be established without opposition from the air.

Two important raids accomplished by the Twelfth in late 1943 were striking evidence of things in store for the Axis. On 24 October, 89 B-17s, 25 B-24s and 36 P-38s bombed the Wiener-Neustadt factory in the first attack on

Another 340th BG machine, B-25J-1 43-4080/'9S' *KNOCKOUT!* was assigned to the 489th BS. Note that its blister gun packs have been removed from the fuselage sides, revealing bare aluminium skinning. The 340th did little strafing in the MTO, resulting in the weighty gun packs being deemed surplus to requirements (*Harry D George Jr*)

German-held Austria from Allied-held airfields in Italy. Then, on 14 November, 91 B-25s of the Twelfth, escorted by 46 P-38s, dropped 144 tons of 500-lb general-purpose bombs (including 52 with 1- to 24-hour-delayed fuses) on Sofia in the first raid to be staged on Bulgaria – a significant mission because of the B-25's limited range.

With the movement of the war away from North Africa, the need for reorganisation of Allied air units in-theatre became necessary. The Fifteenth Air Force was activated on 1 November 1943, and the heavy bombers and long-range fighters of the Twelfth were assigned to it, leaving the latter with fighters, fighter-bombers and medium bombers.

In early December all MTO air forces, including the RAF's Middle Eastern Air Force, merged to become the Mediterranean Allied Air Forces (MAAF). This brought Allied air power in the MTO to its final organisational form, and was followed within a few months by the realisation of its full operational strength. On 1 January 1944, Lt Gen Ira Eaker took over command of MAAF, and on 26 January Maj Gen John Cannon succeeded Gen Spaatz in charge of the Twelfth.

On 15 March 1944 an attempt was made to blast a hole in the main front across Italy at Cassino. This was the first mass use of USAAF heavy bombers (both strategic and tactical units joined in the attack) in close co-operation with the ground troops. A total of 483 'heavies' dropped 1205 tons of bombs on Cassino in a spectacular bombardment that caused worldwide comment. The target was pulverised, but no breakthrough was achieved.

Boasting an impressive mission tally, B-25J *SNOT NOSE* served with the 489th BS/340th BG. While some aeroplane names made sense (this one was probably inspired by the youthful looks of its pilot, Lt W H Brassfield), others made no sense at all (witness *EAGER BEAVER*) (*Harry D George Jr*)

With Allied ground forces stalled at both Anzio and Cassino, it became readily apparent that additional measures were urgently needed to help the troops get to Rome. This led to the Twelfth's participation in Operation *Strangle*, a tactical air offensive that duly resulted in the fall of the first Axis capital, and which set a pattern for all interdiction campaigns to come.

Strangle was an air effort of heretofore unrealised dimensions. It most likely began on 15 March 1944 (the operation was defined by no specific date) at the time of the heavy bombardment of Cassino.

Once MAAF aircraft were committed to the campaign, the accomplishments of the Twelfth Air Force under Gen Cannon in succeeding days exceeded even the most optimistic expectations. By 24 March all rail lines to Rome had been cut, and at no time after this date did any axis road traffic reach the Italian capital. Between 15 March and 11 May, when the ground advance began, MAAF devoted 65,003 effective sorties and 33,104 tons of bombs to this interdiction programme.

When Operation *Coronet* began in May, air and ground forces were given two complementary objectives. The Twelfth and other MAAF units were given the task of 'making it impossible for the enemy to maintain his forces on his present line in Italy in the face of a combined Allied offensive'. This operation began on 24 May, and it saw more than 3200 sorties flown and well over 3000 tons of bombs dropped on roads, railway lines, supply dumps, trucks and tanks. When the Germans fell back in a disorganised rout, the Twelfth kept the pressure on enemy ground transports by concentrating on trucks and soft-skinned vehicles, eventually destroying 6577 examples.

Between 12 May and 22 June, MAAF flew another 72,946 sorties and dropped 51,500 tons of bombs. Seeing the fruit of *Strangle* in the breakthrough of Allied forces and the fall of Rome in early June, Gen Cannon's Twelfth Air Force continued to harass the enemy's communications and supply lines, and at the end of 1944 was engaged in another *Strangle* operation in the Po River Valley, as well as flying close support missions for the Fifth and Eighth Armies.

Then came the Twelfth's Operation *Mallory*, a spectacular bridge-busting campaign using B-25s and B-26s, which caused the destruction of 25 primary road and rail bridges across the Po in 72 hours.

D-Day in southern France (15 August 1944) found the Twelfth Air Force helping to provide aerial cover, softening up coastal defences and hammering at lines of communication. Air mastery over the region was

Not all B-25s lost in the MTO were as a result of enemy action. On 22 March 1944 Mount Vesuvius erupted, showering nearby airfields with tons of hot volcanic ash and brimstone. A significant number of allied aircraft were badly damaged, including this veteran B-25C of the 321st BG. Aside from losing most of its B-25s, the group also suffered significant damage to its maintenance and accommodation facilities (*USAF*)

The unit to which B-25J-1 43-3666 *THE PURPLE SHAFT* was assigned in the MTO remains unknown, but with a serial number ending in '666', it is surprising that this particular Mitchell was not nicknamed 'hell on wheels'! (*USAF*)

487th BS/340th BG B-25J-10 43-27704/'7A' of Capt Jack Ram departs Rimini airfield, in Italy, on 17 August 1944. This aircraft was involved in the attack on the Vichy French battleship *Strasbourg* in Toulon harbour on this day, a heavy barrage of flak thrown up to protect the 702-ft long vessel damaging 27 aircraft, including '7A', but all returned safely to base. The following day B-25s from the 321st BG finished off the *Strasbourg*, a *La Galissonniere* class cruiser and a submarine. The group won its second Distinguished Unit Citation for its actions on 18 August (*via the Author*)

so complete for the initial Allied landings that only one German aeroplane was on hand to oppose some 2700 Allied sorties flown that day.

From May (pre-D-Day in southern France) through to October, the Twelfth's aeroplanes destroyed or damaged 12,190 vehicles, 788 locomotives, 9038 rail cars and 1000+ bridges in the Rhône Valley.

In November the Twelfth took responsibility for the entire Brenner Pass region of north-western Italy, and in Operation *Bingo* neutralised the line between Brennero and Vicenza. The Twelfth's bomb tonnage for 1944 totalled 102,313 tons for all types of targets, and the number of sorties flown reached 193,918. Attacks on the north Italian and Brenner routes reached a climax toward the end of March 1945, when, in one week, nearly 6500 sorties were flown with the loss of 30 aircraft.

In the final burst of action, the Twelfth, and other MAAF units, opened up on 16 April with a mammoth attack, in co-operation with the Fifth Army, aimed at driving the Germans out of northern Italy. The complete surrender of German forces in Italy on 29 April, followed by VE-Day on 8 May, made the coup-de-grace unnecessary.

By war's-end the Twelfth Air Force, and its five B-25 groups, had flown 430,681 sorties, dropped 217,156 tons of ordnance, claimed the destruction of 2857 enemy aircraft and lost 2667 of its own aircraft.

Once the hostilities ended, the Twelfth Air Force was inactivated at Florence, in Italy, on 31 August 1945. It was reactivated at March Field, California, on 17 March 1946, and is still serving with the USAF today at Davis-Monthan Air Force Base, Arizona.

MEDITERRANEAN THEATRE OF OPERATIONS

When USAAF B-25 Mitchell units first began arriving in the MTO in mid 1942, Britain had already been at war with the axis powers for several long years. In North Africa, the RAF and the South African Air Force (SAAF) had been doing their best to stem the steady advancement eastward of German and Italian troops on the ground, but this was becoming increasingly more difficult.

Gen Erwin Rommel's *Afrika Korps* had tracked across the Libyan desert to El Alamein, in Egypt, by July 1942, at which point the only American combat aircraft in the area were a detachment of B-24 Liberators based at Khartoum, in the Sudan.

The previous month British Prime Minister Winston Churchill had requested that the US provide urgent military help because the situation in the Middle East had become parlous. The American government responded with the promise of immediate aircraft reinforcements from India, and the provision of nine USAAF combat groups from the US. All of these aircraft were to be sent to bases in Egypt.

As it happened, the aircraft reinforcements from India turned out to be a handful (nine) of high-time B-17 Flying Fortresses. When they arrived in Cairo on 28 June, Lt Gen Lewis H Brereton, in charge of this 'rag-tag', war-weary fleet of B-17s, ordered the activation of the Middle East Air Force (MEAF), which later became the Ninth Air Force on 12 November 1942.

Too many chiefs and not enough Indians? Mission completed, a B-25C of the 434th BS/12th BG has its left Wright R-2600 radial engine looked at on a damp landing strip in Libya in October 1942. The numerous individuals milling around seem to be a mix of air- and groundcrews (*Norm Taylor Collection*)

The 98th BG (Heavy), 12th BG (M), and the 57th FG had all arrived in the Middle East from the US by mid August 1942, the latter two groups first entering into battle in September with the RAF's Desert Air Force (DAF) in support of Lt Gen Bernard L Montgomery's 8th Army. At this time these three units came under the guidance of the MEAF-cum-Ninth Air Force, but worked in unison with the DAF.

From 24 October through to 5 November, during the hard-fought battle of El Alamein, these units helped the 8th Army prevail against the *Afrika Korps*. Subsequent to that victory, Allied aircraft chased Rommel's forces westward through Libya to Tripoli, on the southern shore of the Mediterranean Sea. In the meantime, additional groups had begun to arrive in the MTO.

The Allied invasion of North Africa (Operation *Torch*) began on 8 November 1942, and during the opening days of the campaign the 12th, 310th and 319th BGs made significant contributions to securing victory. As the operation continued, the 321st and 340th BGs also joined the fray, and these five B-25-equipped groups continued to work in concert in the MTO well into 1944.

As previously mentioned, the 12th BG (nicknamed the 'Earthquakers') had become the first of the Twelfth Air Force's B-25-equipped units to arrive in North Africa – specifically Egypt – in mid August 1942. Three months later both the 310th and 319th BGs had also transferred to North Africa, and by March 1943 the 321st and 340th BGs were also in-theatre.

The month prior to the arrival of the latter two groups had seen British and American air commands in Northwest Africa merge into a single organisation for operational reasons. The Northwest African Air Forces (NAAF) was initially headed by Lt Gen Carl Spaatz, former commander of the Eighth Air Force in England. Most of NAAF's strength was divided between the Northwest African Strategic Air Force (NASAF), under Brig Gen Doolittle, and the Northwest African Tactical Air Force (NATAF), commanded by Air Vice Marshal Sir Arthur Coningham of the RAF, who had led the DAF across North Africa.

USAAF Commander-in-Chief, Gen Henry H 'Hap' Arnold (centre, in the garrison cap) visits the men of the 310th BG in Libya in late 1942. 'Hap' Arnold had wanted to build a large air force prior to the outbreak of World War 2, and by the end of the conflict the USAAF was indeed the largest air arm on the planet. Arnold's dream had come true (*H Aronin via Bob Haney*)

Overall olive drab (OD) camouflaged B-25D-30 42-87461/'7C' of the 487th BS/340th BG blends in well with the multi-hued green and brown terrain below. As Axis fighter defences waned towards the end of the conflict in the MTO, most B-25s serving in-theatre were stripped of their OD paint and flown through to VE-Day in bare metal (*Harry D George Jr*)

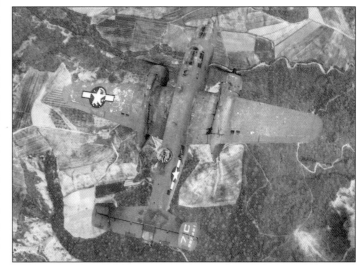

15

B-25J-10 43-36102/'7U' (one of the famous *GI JOE* series aircraft) and B-25J-1 43-27704/'7A' *MY NAKED ASS* of the 487th BS/340th BG head back to their Rimini base following a November 1944 mission to the Brenner Pass
(*USAF via Harry D George Jr*)

Following the Cairo Conference of December 1943, NAAF and Mediterranean Air Command (MAC) merged to form Mediterranean Allied Air Forces (MAAF), which then became a true Allied Theatre Air Headquarters, exercising control of all Allied air forces throughout the MTO.

In January 1944 Gen Ira C Eaker transferred in from the Eighth Air Force in England to take charge of MAAF and its American component, the Army Air Forces/Mediterranean Theatre of Operations (AAF/MTO). Gen Eaker in turn appointed Maj Gen John K Cannon as commander of the Mediterranean Allied Tactical Air Force (MATAF).

In the interim, in November 1943, XII Bomber Command had transformed into the Fifteenth Air Force (Heavy), a strategic bomber force modelled along the lines of the Eighth Air Force and equipped with B-17s and B-24s. Maj Gen Nathan F Twining, who had headed the USAAF's Thirteenth Air Force in the Solomon Islands, took command of the Fifteenth Air Force, and the Mediterranean Allied Strategic Air Force (MASAF).

By this time the MTO had become a subsidiary theatre, and the five Twelfth Air Force Mitchell-equipped bomb groups were performing their duties alongside Fifteenth Air Force units in the Southern and Central European Theatres of Operation (ETO), and in the European-African-Middle Eastern (EAME) Theatre of Operations.

On 19 March 1944, in concert with other heavy and medium bomb groups, the B-25-equipped units helped to launch a different kind of campaign – a co-ordinated air offensive called Operation *Strangle*. Trains and track used to resupply German troops were initially targeted, followed by sorties flown against road transport and shipping. By 11 May MAAF aircraft had flown some 50,000 sorties in support of *Strangle*, and a similar number of flights were achieved during the course of June 1944 alone.

A six-aeroplane box of B-25s from the 486th BS/340th BG unload 24 1000-lb bombs on the lead aircraft's signal. This simultaneous box bombing tactic was widely employed by units within the 340th from mid-1944 onwards (*Harry D George Jr*)

B-25Js from the 310th BG release their 'thousand pounders' over a cloud-obscured Po River Valley in northern Italy in 1944 (*Museum of Flight Collection*)

The crew of B-25J *I'LL TAKE YOU HOME AGAIN KATHLEEN II* of the 486th BS/340th BG prepare to do just that soon after VE-Day (*Mike Haney*)

Throughout the autumn and winter months of 1944-45, MAAF aircraft operated almost unopposed over northern Italy, and in April 1945, after B-25s and other bomber types had decimated what was left of German troops holding out in and around the Po River Valley, the aerial fighting in the Central ETO finally came to an end.

For the 310th, 319th, 321st and 340th BGs, who had fought so hard for so long, it was finally time to go home. The 12th BG had been reassigned to the USAAF's Tenth Air Force in March 1944 for service in the China-Burma-India (CBI) theatre of operations, and the group went home from there.

All five of these outfits had first been baptised under fire in the MTO, and they went on to see action within EAME, Southern and Central ETO and the CBI. Not soon enough for most of the personnel assigned to these groups, 20 battle-weary squadrons flocked together to rightfully become the homeward-bound war heroes that they were. Some men had been in action since day one, while others had only just arrived in the MTO. Many of the long-timers – dubbed 'Lifers' – remained in the service to finish out their respective military careers.

However, most servicemen could not wait to muster out and become civilians once again. Many of these 19-, 20- and 21-year-old 'kids' had children of their own which they had not yet seen. If it had not been for these so-called 'kids', however, who had fought like men, and their much older 22-, 23- and 24-year-old battle-hardened peers, the world we know today might very well have been a very different place.

12th BG (MEDIUM)

The 12th BG (Medium) split off from the 17th BG (Light) in January 1941 at McChord Field, just south of Tacoma, Washington. Constituted on 20 November 1940, it was activated on 15 January 1941 and eventually inactivated on 22 January 1946. During World War 2, the group saw action in the EAME Theatre, Egypt-Libya, Tunisia, Sicily, Naples-Foggia, Rome-Arno, India-Burma, China Defensive and Central Burma. The 12th received two Distinguished Unit Citations for action in North Africa (in October 1942) and Sicily (for its performance on 17 August 1943).

The group's various bases included McChord Field, Washington; Esler Field, Louisiana; Deversoir, Egypt; various Egyptian and Libyan Landing Grounds; Medenine and Hergla, Tunisia; Ponte Olivo and Gerbini, Sicily; Foggia and Gaudo, Italy; and Tezgaon, Pandaveswar, Fenny and Karachi, in India. The 12th was disestablished at Fort Lawton, Washington.

The 12th BG was the first Mitchell-equipped unit to see action in the MTO, initially flying both Inglewood-built B-25Cs and Kansas City-built B-25Ds. After an extremely long ferry flight from Florida by way of the southern route across the Atlantic and the African continent, with numerous refuelling stops, the group arrived at its first base in Egypt (Deversoir) in August 1942. The 12th BG duly made its first attack on Axis targets on the 14th of that same month.

B-25C 41-12831 was one of the original 16 Mitchells flown to the MTO from the USA by the 83rd BS. The 12th BG's four squadrons successfully delivered all 55 of their B-25s from Esler Field, Louisiana, to Deversoir, in Egypt, via the southern route across the Atlantic Ocean and the African continent (*NASM via Bob Haney*)

These B-25Cs, from the 82nd BS (dropping bombs) and 83rd BS, were photographed whilst participating in the 12th BG's first combat mission, on 16 August 1942. Capt Douglas Spawn is at the controls of aircraft '30' (*Alex Adair*)

Nicknamed *MANANA*, and featuring a rendition of 'Donald Duck' in pirate garb, complete with a 'Jolly Roger' flag, this B-25C (serial unknown) served with the 82nd BS during the 12th BG's first months in combat in North Africa. The bomber is seen here en route to a target in Libya in November 1942 (*Norm Taylor Collection*)

The 12th BG served with no less than three US Army Air Forces in World War 2, namely the Ninth, Twelfth and Tenth Air Forces. It also saw action with XII Bomber Command and the Desert Air Force. The Tenth battled the Japanese in the CBI where, from March 1944 until VJ-Day, the 12th BG served following its move from Italy.

The 12th BG controlled four medium bomb squadrons equipped with B-25s throughout World War 2 – the 81st 'Butting Goats', 82nd 'Bulldogs', 83rd 'Black Angels' and 434th 'Cyclones'. The 81st also used the name 'Battering Rams' and the 434th 'Tornados'. The 12th BG flew C-, D-, H- and J-model B-25s.

One of the group's early pilots was Capt Douglas W 'Doug' Spawn of the 82nd BS, who remembered:

'I checked out as first pilot in the B-25 in January 1942 at McChord Field, where the group had 12 to 14 B-25s assigned to it. We flew these to Esler Field, in Louisiana, in February 1942 with no mishaps. At Esler our group was fully equipped with 64 B-25C/Ds, 16 per squadron. They were all painted Desert Pink (mauve), and with that, we knew our destination – Africa!

'In late July 1942 we left Esler and ended up in Deversoir, Egypt, in early August. Two of our squadrons were stationed some 15 miles north of us in Ismailia. Every aeroplane in our group arrived safely in Egypt – a record that I doubt many other groups could claim. We flew overloaded aeroplanes through tropical weather fronts and landed on short runways – sometimes in severe weather.

'In combat, the B-25 proved its worth many, many times over. We flew through desert dust storms and even mountain snowstorms in northern Algeria. The aeroplane was also capable of withstanding severe punishment from enemy flak bursts and fighter gunfire. In most cases the B-25s were able to return to home base. On one mission in particular my aeroplane (Battle Number 33) received more than 100 flak holes, both in the fuselage and wings. It was patched up, and two days later it was in the air again dropping bombs on the enemy.

'The first problem I encountered operating in combat conditions was that desert sand and dust clogged up the carburettor air filters. The

19

sand and dust took its toll on the engines, especially if we removed the air filters for high altitude operations up to 17,000 ft.

'The second problem was caused by the B-25's original engine exhaust pipes (stacks). Each engine had only one large diameter stack, which was good for performance but awful when flying on a clear night – and there were many of these. Flak gunners and fighter pilots could clearly see the exhaust gases (blue and/or orange in colour against the night-time skies) anywhere from 8000 to 10,000 ft, which were our normal operating altitudes. We complained to higher authority about this deadly vulnerability.

'After we lost four of ten B-25s on the night of 14 September 1942, including the aircraft flown by the commander of our group (Col Charles G Goodrich, who was later captured and interned for the duration of the war at *Stalag Luft* 21 – Author) and his crew, we were ordered to fly no more night missions until the exhaust pipe problem was solved. North American Aviation engineers came up with the idea of 'finger-type' exhaust stacks, one for each of the 14 cylinders per engine. Then we resumed night-time operations.

'All in all, I feel that there was no purer combat aeroplane than the B-25 Mitchell. It operated in all theatres – even over heavily defended enemy positions – and returned its crew home with a very low accident rate that was second to none during World War 2.'

The 12th BG was responsible for pioneering many of the tactics used by the five B-25-equipped bomb groups assigned to the MTO. The following explanation of these tactics is based on information gleaned by the author from a period account written by Capt Henry L Colman of the 434th BS.

Operations began in August 1942 from Kabrit, Deversoir and Ismailia, all three landing grounds being sited near the Suez Canal.

B-25C-1 41-13237 of the 82nd BS races its shadow, and five others from its box formation, across the Sahara Desert in late 1942. The bomber is finished in standard Desert Pink and Neutral Gray, and bears the usual North African theatre marking of an RAF fin flash on inner and outer vertical tail surfaces. The 82nd BS, along with sister-squadron the 81st BS, detached from the 12th BG in February 1943 to support the First Army in Algeria, leaving the 83rd and 434th BSs to soldier on with the Eighth Army in Tripoli (*USAF via Bob Wilson*)

41-13237's combat career with the 12th BG did not last much beyond the sortie featured in the photograph above, as this shot clearly shows. Its pilot was forced to make a wheels-up belly landing (little more than a controlled crash, judging by the damage visible in this photo) at LG 88, in Egypt, after the bomber suffered total hydraulic failure (*USAF via Bob Wilson*)

The 12th moved steadily westward behind the US Eighth Army, conducting sorties in support of its advance. At the time this account was compiled in the summer of 1943, the group was based near Nabaul, on Cape Bon.

NIGHT BOMBING TACTICS

'In the summer of 1942, when the Eighth Army and Rommel's forces were facing each other at El Alamein, the B-25s of the 12th BG were used almost exclusively for night-time bombardment missions. Targets included railroad yards, airdromes, dispersal areas, harbour facilities, warehouses, motorised transport and troop concentrations, docks and vessels in harbours – all behind enemy lines.

'Between 24 and 48 aircraft were despatched on these night missions. There was no formation flying at night, the aircraft being despatched individually from the home landing ground (LG) at five-minute intervals. Each aircraft was on its own. Flight to within 50 miles of the target was usually made under 1000 ft, and never over 3000 ft, so as to stay off the enemy radar screens as long as possible. The aircraft climbed to 8000-9000 ft before the bombing approach. The bombs used were British 250- and 300-lb general purpose (GP) bombs, some of which were fitted with nose-rods to increase the area of lethal effect.

'Preceding the initial attack upon a target by the B-25s, RAF Albacores and Wellingtons would usually drop flares over the target area.

'Most of the targets were on, or close to, the coast of the Mediterranean Sea. The usual procedure was for the B-25s to swing out over the Nile River Delta and then fly over the Mediterranean, turning in to the target from the sea.

'Target times were prearranged for each B-25. Each pilot was briefed to release his bombs on the target within a specific very few seconds. The attack plan was worked out so that individual aircraft could make as many as four runs over the target, the exact number of runs being prearranged. After the initial bombing run, a B-25 was to fly away from the target on a certain heading, for a certain length of time, then double back, hitting the target again within another time bracket of a very few seconds. In the meantime, between the two runs of this first aircraft, another aircraft came in, made its first run and flew away from the target on another course. After the first aircraft had completed its second attack, and at about the time the second aircraft was turning to come back over the target for its second pass, a third aircraft was making its first attack. After the third aircraft had completed its initial bombing run, the second aircraft followed with its second pass. And so it went.

Boasting 30+ mission symbols below the cockpit, an anonymous 83rd BS B-25C roars down the runway at LG 88 at the start of yet another combat sortie in late 1942. The Allies utilised numerous Landing Grounds in the Sahara Desert during the North African campaign, these sites being declared operational simply by ensuring that a supply of full 55-gallon fuel drums was on hand and sufficient tents erected (*USAF*)

'As can be seen, this plan of attack, involving the operation of as many as 48 aircraft in one night over the same target, making several individual passes, involved strict adherence by all pilots to a split-second timing schedule.

'Because the calibre and intensity of anti-aircraft (AA) artillery fire varied so greatly from night-to-night and target-to-target, it was impossible to brief the pilots for a rigid bombing approach altitude. Pilots were allowed to be governed by the flak conditions encountered, and to use their own judgement on the altitudes they should fly over defended areas. It was because of this that the system of exact target times and definite compass headings was adopted for the attacking B-25s. Most enemy night opposition was AA artillery fire. Only a few nightfighters were encountered, and no crew was certain that a night fighter ever attacked it.

'Enemy AA artillery was accurate and intense at important points such as Mersa Matruh, El Daba and Tobruk. Enemy searchlights and AA artillery was believed to be co-ordinated and controlled by radio. The basic evasive tactics of the B-25s against AA artillery fire and searchlights were gradual turns right and left and gradual climbing and diving manoeuvres.

'After the breakthrough at El Alamein, when the landing fields and dispersal areas previously bombed by B-25s were examined, there were few aircraft shelters that had not been damaged. Many burned-out aircraft were found in wrecked shelters. It is estimated that B-25s, and other RAF and US aircraft, destroyed several hundred enemy aircraft on the ground whilst providing air support for the El Alamein breakthrough.

This B-25C (serial unknown) of the 82nd BS suffered an engine failure deep over the Mediterranean while carrying a full bomb load, forcing the pilot to ditch. A single engine did not provide enough power to keep a fully manned and nearly fully fuelled Mitchell aloft, especially if that same aircraft was carrying eight 500-lb bombs. No matter what model of B-25 crews flew in the MTO, the saying, 'we're only as good as our engines' was often proven true (*12th BG Association, AFFTC/HO via Frederick A Johnsen*)

B-25C 41-12829 (foreground) saw service both with the 12th and 340th BGs in North Africa. It is seen here in early 1943 whilst flying with the 81st BS. Formating with the bomber is B-25C 41-12864 of the 83rd BS (*USAF via Bob Haney*)

PATTERN BOMBING BY DAY

'When the Eighth Army Desert Air Force (DAF) got moving in October 1942, the B-25s of the 12th BG were switched over from night-time to daytime bombing. During daylight, the B-25s operated invariably in formations of 18 – three six-ship boxes. The aircraft

flew in tight, shallow V-formation. They flew in three flights of six, broken down into two elements of three in each flight. B-25s in each element flew from a few feet to 25 ft apart. The rear element flew 25 to 50 ft above or below the lead element to stay out of the propeller-wash.

'Each flight flew not more than 50 yards apart, and sometimes much closer, or in tight formation. It was customary for the lead flight to be lowest, and the other two higher. Whether the left or right flight was highest depended upon the direction of the turn to be made away from the target area. The flight that had to make the greatest turn was placed highest.

'In their initial daylight combat flights in formation, the B-25s were "broken in" by formations of RAF Douglas A-20 Havoc and Martin A-30 Baltimore light-attack bombers. Missions were flown with A-20s or Baltimores comprising the lead flight. By late October 1942, however, B-25 pilots had perfected formation flying, and during the advance across the desert, they were capable of operating in full 18-aeroplane formations.

'The type of attack most frequently used by the B-25s during daylight was pattern bombing (better known as carpet bombing today – Author). This method was adopted because, in most cases, the targets were airdromes, dispersal areas, troop concentrations and the like, in which there was no individual objective that warranted precision (specific target) bombing. Rather, these areas contained many targets, situated close to one another, all of which were equally important to destroy. Therefore, far more damage was generated in the long run by covering the area with a pattern (or carpet) of bombs. The pattern of destruction was always worked out with geometric precision in advance, and upon it the whole plan for the formation bombing approach was made.

'As at night, approach to the target was made at low level, with a gradual climb to the point where the bombing approach commenced at between 6500 and 8500 ft, the actual altitude depending on the weather. Immediately prior to the approach, the formation (flight) leader signalled the formation to loosen up and space itself according to a prearranged plan based on the size and nature of the target.

B-25C 41-12869, flown by the 82nd BS's Capt Doug Spawn, heads for the Axis-held Mareth Line, in Tunisia, on 9 January 1943. Behind the Mitchells are Baltimore IIIs of the RAF's No 232 Wing, and partially obscured by 41-12869's mid upper turret is a P-40K of the 57th FG. Experienced bomber units from the RAF and SAAF were instrumental in helping the 12th BG earn its combat 'spurs' (*NASM via Bob Haney*)

The crew of the 12th BG's *DESERT WARRIOR* (B-25C 41-12860) pose at Bolling Field, Washington DC, in mid-summer 1943. A high-mission B-25 in the MTO when sent back to the US on a War Bond drive in the spring of 1943, 41-12860's crew consisted of (from left to right), back row, pilot Capt Ralph Lower (82nd BS), co-pilot 1Lt Clarence Seaman (81st BS), navigator 1Lt Floyd Pond (434th BS) and bombardier 1Lt Theodore Tate (83rd BS). Front row (left to right) gunner S/Sgt James Garfolo (83rd BS), radioman/gunner Flg Off Anthony Martin (82nd BS, and ex-RCAF) and crew chief M/Sgt John Dawdy (81st BS)
(*Paul Peck via Bob Haney*)

Below left
DESERT WARRIOR is seen from the right side while still in North Africa. Its MTO career was most impressive, the bomber flying 73 combat missions totalling 191 combat hours. During the course of these sorties, the B-25 dropped over 90 tons of bombs and its gunners were credited with the destruction of three enemy fighters. All of these details were contained within the scroll painted below the cockpit, while the large white panel that surrounded the nose glazing listed the various decorations awarded to the crews that flew 41-12860
(*USAF via Bob Wilson*)

Below
Although the artwork on 41-12860's nose looks new, the rest of the aeroplane appears more combat weary
(*AFFTC/HO via F Johnson*)

'The distances between B-25s in the element, between each element and between the three flights were worked out with a view to covering the target with a pattern of bombs hitting not more than 50 ft apart. Aircraft released their bombs when the formation leader dropped his.

'In bombing motorised tank (MT) columns, the bombing approach was made at an angle of between 20 and 30 degrees, so that the bombing pattern would form a parallelogram. It was possible to pattern bomb MT columns because in retreat, Rommel's fleeing army was moving along in three or more parallel lines close to each other at the same time. The area bounded by the parallelogram was the area the B-25s attempted to cover with their formation pattern bombing. The bombs were aimed short and over the MT columns, as well as on them. This is because the columns would attempt to disperse when they sighted the attacking bombers. Vehicles and troops could not get very far, but generally some were able to move off a little to both sides.

'By affecting the bomb pattern as previously described, the B-25s hit troops, tanks and trucks that otherwise would have escaped. The parallelogram pattern was adopted because it gave the aircraft a longer dropping time over the target. The B-25 crews found that when toggling their bombs at approximately half-second intervals, they could put an average of two more bombs per aircraft into the target than if they attacked the columns from a direct 90-degree angle.

'Rommel's MT columns were well protected with mobile light and heavy AA artillery. The 88 mm guns of the 15th and 21st Panzer Divisions were especially feared.

'Until they reached Tunisia, the B-25s were given protective cover by USAAF P-40s. Protection was usually on the flanks, above and sometimes behind. Crews state that there was never a time when a bomber that had been hit and forced to leave the formation was not protected by at least two P-40s. They stress that tight formations were necessary, not only to achieve maximum defensive firepower, but also so that the fighter escorts did not have to disperse their protection.

'The enemy fighters that were encountered were of the best the axis had at the time. These included German Messerschmitt Me 109s, Focke-Wulf FW 190s and Italian Macchi 200s, with the Me 109s featuring most prominently of the three types encountered.

'The most typical initial enemy fighter attack was frontal – from above and out of the sun. Many B-25 missions were flown in the late

B-25C 41-13120 was assigned to Capt George Simmons of the 434th BS whilst the unit was based at Sfax, in Tunisia, in the spring of 1943. This photograph was taken on 6 May that same year, when 41-13120 was one of 18 B-25s that the unit succeeded in launching on a navigation-training mission to Castel Benito and back – the 83rd BS also contributed nine Mitchells to this operational exercise. Two days later 41-13120 was involved in a combat mission against dispersed enemy aircraft on Pantelleria island (*Norm Taylor Collection*)

afternoon when they were forced to fly westward into the sun. Enemy aircraft often dived out of the sun in elements of three from 12 o'clock, fanning out and making individual attacks from the 12 o'clock, 2 o'clock and 10 o'clock positions. Usually, then, the number one aircraft pulls up a little while the number two aircraft swings out to the left, does a wingover, and makes a pass at the number two aircraft in the lead element of B-25s from 2 o'clock.

This 'plain Jane' B-25C was assigned to the 83rd BS at Gambut, in Libya, in November 1942. All 1625 C-model Mitchells built by North American Aviation were constructed at the company's huge Inglewood, California, facility (*Norm Taylor Collection*)

'The number three enemy aircraft dives under the formation and away after making its pass. Just as the number three enemy fighter begins its pass from the side at 2 o'clock, the number one enemy aircraft makes a direct diving pass at the lead B-25. The number one enemy fighter zooms over the formation, away and up again after another pass when it's out of range. In the meantime, the number three enemy fighter, acting simultaneously with enemy fighter number two, has crossed over to the right and above number two going the other way, and has made the same type of attack as number two, but from 10 o'clock and on B-25 number three. Enemy fighter number three also dives away under the bomber formation.

PRECISION BOMBING

'When on a precision bombing mission, B-25 tactics were the same as for pattern bombing, except that each aircraft made an individual run over the target, coming back into formation immediately after the attack. Precision bombing targets included communication centres, strong points in the Mareth line, fuel dumps, coastal defence gun emplacements at Pantelleria and enemy naval vessels. Bombs varied from 250- to 1000-lb general purpose and, in most cases, the Estoppey D-8 bombsight was used.'

There were three well-known bombsights used in World War 2 – the Sperry S-1, the famed Norden M-9 and the Estoppey D-8. The latter, mentioned above, was very simple to operate. It had a set of wire-type sighting elements that were hand-driven to establish synchronisation with relative target movement. Time of fall was set into a timing mechanism to compute the ground speed, thus solving the bombing problem. Provisions were made to set in drift and angle and trail. The sight was stabilised through a pendulum and dashpot mounting system. According to Tech Order No 11-30-5, dated 25 July 1942;

'Stabilisation of the D-8 is of the pendulum type, damped by two dash pots at right angles to each other. The pendulum stabilising mechanism allows roughly a six-degree deviation from the vertical.'

Briefly, the D-8 was the brainchild of George Estoppey, a civilian employee of Swiss origin who came to McCook Field Engineering Division in July 1921. The D-8 was put into quantity production by the National Cash Register Company in 1939 due to the critical shortage of bombsights at this time, but had been discontinued by October 1943 when the Norden M-9 became the standard sighting device.

Perhaps the most outstanding example of precision bombing performed by the B-25 in the MTO was the destruction of Rommel's main communications centre at El Alamein, located underground just behind the German lines, on 24 October 1942. First located by an RAF Wellington equipped with an externally mounted magnetic ring-link detection system, the centre's air-search radar was jammed by additional Wellingtons that braved intense AA artillery fire whilst continuously circling the target for a full 24 hours prior to the early morning raid. The B-25s attacked at dawn on the 24th in three formations of six, spaced at 15-minute intervals. They scored at least four or five direct hits on the 150 x 150-ft target, and all radio traffic from this location immediately ceased.

A few days later, after the Eighth Army had advanced, examination of the communications centre showed it to be completely destroyed. This accomplishment was highly important to the Allied effort, since it denied to Rommel his quickest means of communicating with his far-flung units just at the time when he needed it most.

Towards the end of the North African campaign, when the 12th BG was based near the east coast of Tunisia, the enemy was running ships in and out of jetties on Cape Bon. If reconnaissance disclosed that vessels were coming in, the 12th always let them berth first in order to get a crack at the ships when they were stationary, rather than underway at sea. These attacks were usually carried out by elements of three aircraft flying at between 5000 and 7000 ft, weather permitting.

Two of the B-25s would initiate the attack by making co-ordinated runs that saw one bomber laying its ordnance diagonally across the stern from one direction, and the other dropping its bombs diagonally across the stern from another direction, thus splitting the defensive gunfire. The third B-25 would follow up these attacks seconds later running across either the bow or the stern.

Mitchells were sent on several sea sweeps off Cape Bon in areas where there was known to be no friendly shipping. These sweeps were usually carried out at sundown because at this time, about two months before the end of the campaign, enemy shipping was moving out from Tunisian harbours into the Straits of Sicily at the end of each day. Formations were not flown during these sorties, individual B-25s instead being given a certain search area. They located nothing big, but several small ships were sunk by 'lone wolves', which always attacked diagonally across the stern or bow, releasing their bombs from about 6000 ft.

OTHER HIGHLIGHTS

B-25 crews were especially pleased with the results of their attacks on columns of enemy tanks. As the Eighth Army captured more ground, personnel from the 12th BG's four B-25 units were able to

B-25H-10 43-5104 *BONES* of the 82nd BS was the 1000th, and last, H-model built – it was also the final Mitchell constructed in California. Once the bomber had been signed by the numerous workers that had put it together, 43-5104 was shipped off to the MTO, where it is seen dropping 1000-lb bombs on a road in northern Italy
(*Early Garrett via Bob Haney*)

examine the results of these attacks for themselves. They found many burned-out tanks with their tread/tracks blown off and the crews roasted alive within. Further examination showed that some of the Panzers had apparently been set alight by near misses, which had ruptured their fuel tanks, causing an immediate and intense fire. And they were in a highly flammable state, since the tanks were operating a long way from their bases and field depots, and were laden down with significant quantities of extra fuel. Moreover, in most cases, the Panzers' unfired shells would also explode.

When the Tunisian show was over, two incidents occurred that revealed just how mission effective the B-25 crews had become in less than a year of combat.

Crews from one of the units were dining at the officers' club in Tunis when a group of New Zealand infantrymen heard they were in town. These were the same men for whom the B-25s – hitting enemy armour and mobilised infantry – had blasted a path through the Axis frontline in the El Hamma area. The New Zealanders went to the club and asked for the officers, then seized them, gave joyous thanks for what they had done, hoisted them onto their shoulders and staged a private victory parade.

The second incident occurred when a group of German prisoners of war were brought to the B-25 landing ground at Cape Bon. They took one look at the aircraft and exclaimed, 'Mitchells! Ach, Der Lieber! Acht Zehn Roter Teuflen!' The Germans had been so amazed at the fact that exactly 18 B-25s had attacked them day after day, maintaining a tight formation in the face of intense AA artillery fire, that they had nicknamed them '18 Red Devils'.

After moving from North Africa to Sicily in mid 1943, the 12th BG pounded axis targets in southern France and southern Italy.

In March 1944 the group packed up and moved from Italy to eastern India, where it was assigned to the Tenth Air Force. Here, the 12th BG primarily operated against the Japanese in Burma, with a few excursions into China. In addition to bombing communication sites and other military installations, the group also delivered ammunition to Allied forces at Imphal.

In the summer of 1945 the 12th BG began its conversion onto the A-26 Invader for the ongoing Allied push towards Japan's home islands. However, on 2 September 1945 the Japanese surrendered, and the group never got to fly a combat mission with the formidable A-26. The 12th returned to the US in December 1945, and the group was duly inactivated on 22 January 1946.

The 12th BG was not replaced within the Twelfth Air Force's 57th BW, which finished the war with four B-25-equipped groups – the 310th, 319th, 321st and 340th.

The first to arrive in the MTO in August 1942, the 12th BG had also been the first to leave.

This war-weary B-25C from the 12th BG was photographed on short finals in Italy in early 1944, just weeks prior to the group's move to India. B-25C/Ds were built with retractable ventral turrets, fitted with twin 0.50-cal machine guns. When the reality of combat proved the near uselessness of the turret, and the hazardous conditions facing those who manned it, the fitting was removed (*Norm Taylor Collection*)

310th BG (MEDIUM)

The 310th BG (M) was the fourth group equipped with the B-25 to arrive in the MTO, its four squadrons being the 379th, 380th, 381st and 428th BSs. Constituted on 28 January 1942, the 310th was activated on 15 March 1942 and inactivated on 12 September 1945. It saw action in the EAME Theatre, Tunisia, Sicily, Naples-Foggia, Rome-Arno, southern France, the north Apennines, central Europe and the Po River Valley. The group received two Distinguished Unit Citations, one on 27 August 1943 for action in Italy, and the second on 10 March 1945 for its accomplishments at Ora, again in Italy.

The 310th was based at Davis-Monthan Field, Arizona; Jackson Army Air Base and Key Field, Mississippi; Columbia Army Air Base, Walterboro and Greenville Army Air Base, South Carolina; Mediouna, French Morocco; Telergma and Berteaux, Algeria; Der el Koudia and Menzel Temime, Tunisia; Philippeville, Algeria; Ghisonaccia, Corsica; and Fano and Pomigliano, Italy.

The group initially sent two (379th and 428th BSs) of its four squadrons to the MTO in November 1942, these units routing via England, and arriving in Casablanca on the 12th.

Following considerable assistance from the battle-hardened RAF and Free French Air Force, the 310th mounted its first offensive on 2 December 1942 when an eight-ship formation (four from the 379th and four from the 428th) hit an ammunition dump near Gabes, in Tunisia. Four days later the 310th flew its second mission, bombing the airfield at Sidi Ahmed, near Biserte. During the raid a B-25 from the 379th was lost, along with its six-man crew.

On 14 December the six remaining aircraft (one had crash-landed at the group's Mediouna base after returning from a mission to Sousse harbour, in Tunisia) moved temporarily to Telergma while work continued on the group's more permanent facility at Berteaux. It was around this time that nine more aircraft – three from the 380th and six from the 381st – arrived at Telergma. At last all four squadrons within the group were together, albeit with a very limited number (15) of Mitchells.

B-25C-1 41-13070 of the 310th BG flies low over the Mediterranean near Berteaux, Morocco, en route to its target. When this photograph was taken in early 1943 the group had yet to apply its distinctive tail markings, which consisted of a yellow band flanked by individual squadron colours – white for the 379th, red for the 380th, blue for the 381st and yellow for the 428th. Without such a marking, it is virtually impossible to work out which unit this particular Mitchell belonged to (*USAF*)

On 30 December each squadron was represented for the first time when a 12-aeroplane mission was sent to bomb the marshalling yards at Sousse. This operation, along with the preceding seven missions, were for the most part quite successful. Yet one aeroplane had been lost and another crash-landed.

In the meantime, work continued apace at nearby Berteaux, with the runway being created by scraping and grading out a flat winter wheat field set between low hills. In January 1943 the group moved-in, but the runway wasn't actually 'finished' until a number of B-25s had already landed and taken off from it.

Operating against Axis airfields in Tunisia and the sea-lanes from Sicily to harbours on the Mediterranean coast, the 310th flew 28 missions in January. Three B-25s and two crews were lost, but in return the group claimed 12 aircraft destroyed and two merchant ships and two naval vessels sunk. Mission after mission followed in February, and the 310th paid the price. Five aircraft and crews were lost during the first ten days of the month – four on 8 February alone while bombing Gabes airfield. All had fallen victim to flak.

A fifth Mitchell was also badly damaged over Gabes on the 8th, 381st B-25C *POTCH-A-GALOOP*, flown by Lt Eric Linden, limping away from the target area with its bomb-bay doors frozen open. It also had its lower gun turret stuck in the extended position, no working instruments in the cockpit and damaged flight control surfaces. Despite the aeroplane being barely flyable, Lt Linden managed to perform a spectacular crash-landing at Berteaux, saving his crew.

On three consecutive days – 21, 22 and 23 February – six aircraft and five crews were lost. February proved to be a terrible month for combat casualties, with the 310th losing eleven aircraft and ten crews.

The weather turned bad in March, and only three sea-sweeps were flown in the first six days, but not one bomb was dropped. On the 7th, however, six aircraft on a sea-sweep spotted and attacked a convoy. A large freighter was left sinking and another smaller freighter and two auxiliary vessels were sunk. All six aircraft returned to base with varying degrees of flak damage.

The 310th lost yet another aeroplane and its crew on 12 March, although the day's sea-sweep produced great results. A convoy of 12 Seibel ferries had been attacked, three of which were sunk and three left badly damaged or sinking.

From the middle to the end of March, the 310th's sister group, the 321st, arrived in-theatre and was deployed at Ain M'lila, some 10-12 kilometres from the 310th's base at Berteaux. Following the 12 March convoy attack, the weather deteriorated once again, and the 310th managed to fly just another nine missions for the rest of the month, dropping bombs on just five of them. One aeroplane, and its crew, was lost.

The next significant action for the group occurred on 10 April, when a sea-sweep turned into a veritable 'turkey shoot'. As it happened, 18 B-25s, loaded with eight 500-lb bombs apiece, were looking for shipping targets but instead found a large formation of Luftwaffe transports off Cape Bon. The aerial convoy was made up of 25 Ju 52/3ms, accompanied by a number of Me 410s, Ju 87s and Ju 88s. In the vanguard of the USAAF attack were the 24 escorting P-38s, but the B-25 crews also joined in by flying back and forth along the sides of the formation firing every 0.50-cal gun they had. Gunners from the 310th claimed ten Ju 52/3ms and one Ju 88, while the P-38s accounted for another 14, plus a lone Bf 109 intercepted off Biserte on the way home.

Wanting 'a piece of the action', a number of B-25 pilots and co-pilots took turns at the controls, leaving the spare man to crawl down into the nose and fire the 0.50-cal guns fitted in the bombardier's compartment.

In April 1943 the 310th flew 19 missions, sinking three freighters and damaging two others. It also destroyed 19 enemy aircraft. But this success came at a high price, for five B-25s and their crews were lost.

A further 18 missions were flown in May, and six aircraft and three crews lost. However, by the end of the month the group had inflicted serious damage on Axis shipping and destroyed 48 aircraft – both in the air and on the ground.

On 5-6 June the 310th moved from Berteaux to Souk el Arba ('King's Cross'), in Algeria, this site being some 150 miles further east, but closer to prime Axis targets in the north. By the end of June the group had flown another 17 missions, losing two more B-25s. The 310th had now flown an overall total of 116 missions, losing 28 aircraft and 42 crewmen to enemy action.

In July the group racked up 706 sorties during 19 missions flown by all four squadrons, and lost six more aircraft – four B-25s, and their crews, to enemy fire, and two Mitchells scrapped after crash landing.

On 17 August Sicily fell, and the group was now turned loose on targets on the Italian mainland. One of these missions against the marshalling yard at Benevento, in the Naples/Salerno area, would cost the 310th dearly. As 36 B-25s struggled to attain cruising altitude over the Mediterranean, prior to crossing the Italian coast just north-east of Naples, they were attacked by 50 enemy aircraft. The B-25s had to fend off a mixed gaggle of German Bf 109s and Fw 190s and Italian Reggiane Re 2001s and Macchi C.202s. Although bracketed by 'friendly' flak aimed at the B-25s, axis fighters pressed home their attacks and downed three Mitchells over the target. Two more were badly damaged, but were able to make it home.

Despite the losses suffered at Benevento, the 310th was able to put up 60 aircraft just three days later. August ended with another mission against a marshalling yard, although this time the target was

The original print of this photo had the following note penned on the back, written by 310th BG pilot, O B Taylor;

'13 November 1943, Mariut Airport, Alexandria. This photo was taken about 15 minutes after the ship started sinking. Field is essentially quicksand where not paved, which I did not know when I swung out to avoid a crew of "working" Arabs. Left wheel dug in the instant it left the pavement, plane swung around 180° to left. Not able to leave until 17 November after getting new wheel from Cairo. Wheels had eroded almost completely away in the salt-saturated soil' (O B Taylor)

B-25C-5 42-53451 *WORTH FIGHTING FOR* served with the 380th BS in 1942-43. Note the bomber's horizontal yellow bands just above the aircraft's serial number on each of its vertical tail sections. This marking was adopted by the group in April 1943. The B-25 also features an outlined (in either yellow or red) national marking (*NASM via Bob Haney*)

A solid-nose B-25J, armed with eight 0.50 cal machine guns, proved to be a most effective gunnery platform for low-level strafing runs against ships. With another four blister pack 'fifties' (two on either side of the fuselage) and two top turret 'fifties', the J-model could bring 14 forward-firing 0.50 cal machine guns to bear (*USAF*)

situated in the port town of Civitavécchia, west of Rome.

Some 14 missions had been flown by the 310th during August, and four aircraft and crews had been lost. Three more B-25s were written off in crash-landings upon returning to base.

The 310th flew a further 22 missions in September, losing seven B-25s and six crews. Significantly, on the 25th a mission had been flown that had seen the Mitchells loaded with four 1000-lb bombs rather than eight 500 'pounders'. This was the first time such a load had been dropped in anger.

The 184th, and last, bombing mission flown by the 310th from North Africa was undertaken on 31 October, when Civitavécchia was attacked once again. Two aircraft and their crews were lost in October.

November 1943 saw the group receive its first B-25Gs, equipped with a single 75 mm cannon in a 'solid' nose fairing. These were immediately put to use in sea-sweeps of the Dodecanese Islands, which had been occupied by Italian forces until liberated by the British on 8 September. During November some 58 75 mm rounds were fired at 14 vessels, with a destroyer and two E-boats being hit and most likely sunk. Not a single B-25 was lost during this month, and for the first time since December 1942 not one bomb was dropped.

In December training at Philippeville, in Algeria, continued in preparation for the 310th's move to Corsica. And while the 379th continued to operate out of Gambut, in Libya, the 380th, 381st and 428th trained. By year-end, the group's mission tally since its MTO debut had increased to 223. Some 44 aircraft and 35 combat crews (many of whom were PoWs) had been lost to enemy action.

Come January 1944, the 310th still had only one of its squadrons – the 379th 'Wetzel's Weasels' – fighting the axis. Flying out of Gambut, its B-25Gs were for the most part attacking shipping in the eastern Mediterranean. The first 12 B-25s from the 310th arrived at Corsica's Ghisonaccia airfield on 10 January 1944 – the group was now based just 85 miles from the west coast of Italy. Its first mission was flown three days later, when a sea-sweep of the southern coast of France failed to locate any Axis vessels. The next day another sweep of the same area located an oil tanker off Cannes, and this was set alight.

From 15 January onwards, the group started flying three to four missions per day (usually comprising six aircraft in a box per mission) against various targets – both shipping and ports.

An Allied invasion force landed at Nettuno and Anzio on 22 January, effectively bypassing the German forces stubbornly defending Cassino against Allied armies that had been inching their way northward following the Salerno landings in September 1943. Day after day, three of the 310th's four squadrons (the 379th was still engaged in the eastern Mediterranean, flying from Gambut) continued their interdiction efforts over the Tyrrhenian and Ligurian Seas. By the end of the month the group had flown 231 sorties in 48 missions, sinking 15 vessels and shooting down two aeroplanes. One B-25 was lost in a crash-landing at Ghisonaccia after it had returned from a sea-sweep.

The 379th BS remained at Gambut into February 1944, hitting targets in the eastern Mediterranean and Aegean Seas in and around the German-occupied Greek islands of the Dodecanese chain. The month got off to a bad start for the unit when, on the 1st, two out of a formation of four B-25Gs were lost near the island of Leros. The 379th flew its last mission from Gambut on 22 February, after which it moved to Corsica to rejoin the rest of the group.

During February 1944 the 310th BG flew 59 missions, dropped 1650 tons of bombs and fired a staggering 1100 75 mm cannon and 102,000 0.50-cal machine gun rounds. It also lost three aeroplanes and their crews.

The group joined the 57th BW, Twelfth Air Force, on 15 March, although it remained at Ghisonaccia. At this time, the 57th controlled four battle-hardened groups equipped with B-25s.

March had seen the 310th BG complete 27 missions (698 sorties) and destroy 50 assorted naval vessels and railway tracks and trains, as well as causing serious damage to roads and bridges. But another three aircraft and their crews were lost in action.

Bad weather in April saw the the 310th's mission tally drop to 23, yet the month was counted as one of the group's most productive, for it played a big part in Operation *Strangle* – the campaign responsible for severing virtually all rail links to Rome from the north.

The first ten days of May saw the group going after railway bridges between Chiusi and Orvieto, in Italy. With the 310th now devoting its attention to targets on land, all of its remaining B-25G/Hs were phased out of squadron service. The group now operated B-25C/D/Js, with the C- and D-models being somewhat war-weary. The 'factory fresh' B-25Js, on the other hand, gleamed in their unpainted natural metal finish (these aircraft had only arrived in late April), and they had to be covered with camouflage netting when on the ground.

Monte Cassino fell at last on 18 May 1944, and the road to Rome was finally open. Between 22-31 May, the group flew 21 missions (355 sorties), and during the last two of these nearly 8000 fragmentation ('frag') bombs were dropped with devastating effect on two enemy troop concentrations located just south of Rome.

The group completed a further 52 missions in June, which saw 12 railway bridges destroyed or damaged. The 310th lost five aircraft over the target and five more were written off after limping home damaged – 38 other B-25s suffered less serious flak damage.

The second stage of Operation *Diadem* commenced in July 1944, and rail targets (bridges, tunnels and trains) were attacked throughout the Po River Valley. The 310th BG flew its 500th mission during the month, making it the most combat-experienced B-25 bomb group in the MTO. Although the 310th suffered no losses during July's 31 missions, a number of aircraft (almost all B-25Js) suffered damage. The

This 379th BS B-25G was christened *Pisonya* – a most appropriate name for a dedicated war fighting aircraft. It is debatable whether the enemy understood what this sobriquet meant, however
(*G Rittenhouse via Bob Haney*)

group also participated in Operation *Mallory Major*, which was mounted in an effort to destroy all rail and road bridges.

In August 1944 the 310th took part in Operation *Anvil* (later renamed *Dragoon*), which was instigated to eliminate railway bridges, trains, marshalling yards, radar installations and the like in France's Rhône Valley, and along its Mediterranean coast. The group flew 61 missions in August, losing two B-25Js and their crews to heavy flak. It had now completed 582 missions since December 1942.

In September 1944 the group completed a further 47 missions, losing three aircraft and their crews. On the 22nd of the month, six separate missions involving 106 aircraft had been generated, and almost 10,000 20-lb 'frag' (anti-personnel) bombs had been dropped, as well as another 200 tons of 500- and 1000-lb bombs.

In October Col Peter H Remington (from the 321st BG) replaced Col Anthony G Hunter as group CO, the latter having been with the 310th since June 1942. Hunter, in turn, moved up to 57th BW headquarters. Between 1-20 October the group flew 24 missions, but bad weather then halted any further sorties until 4 November, when the 310th resumed its attacks on railway targets.

The group would fly 52 missions and lose three B-25s and their crews during November. In the middle of the month Yugoslavian targets were also attacked by the 310th for the first time, with three rail and two road bridges being knocked out. Despite this success, the group never again ventured into Yugoslavia.

Now sporting the aforementioned colour schemes on their tails, an assorted collection of OD and natural metal B-25Js from the 310th BG head north-west across the Ligurian Sea for their assigned targets in southern France in 1944 (*USAF*)

B-25J-1 43-27475 is just moments away from returning to the 310th BG's Fano base on the Adriatic coast in late 1944. Note that this machine lacks both its upper turret and its nose-mounted 0.50 cal machine gun (*Norm Taylor Collection*)

In December 1944 the 310th completed 43 missions, taking its overall wartime tally to 748. It also lost four aircraft. During the course of the month SHORAN (SHOrt RANge navigation) was employed by the group for the first time. The system used an onboard computer to feed precision navigation data to the crew from pulsed transmissions sent out from two or more fixed stations. This meant that crews could now blind bomb targets previously masked by bad weather.

The 310th flew 43 missions on the 19 days in January 1945 that weather did not hinder combat operations. February proved marginally more successful, with the group completing 54 missions in 21 days. Many aircraft were damaged but only one was lost, the B-25 crashing on take-off from Ghisonaccia – one of its fuel tanks caught fire and its eight 500-lb bombs exploded. Astoundingly, the crew escaped unharmed and none of the nearby ground personnel were hurt.

During March the 310th BG recorded the following milestones – 15,000 individual sorties, 50,000 combat hours and 29,000 tons of bombs dropped. Sixty-one missions were completed during the 24 days of the month deemed good enough for flying. And it was during one of these missions in late March (a SHORAN attack on a railway bridge at Pordenone) that the group was attacked by 20 Bf 109s and Fw 190s. B-25 gunners downed four fighters, but a single bomber was lost – the group's first loss to an Axis aircraft since September 1943.

Between 4-15 April the group moved from Ghisonaccia to Fano, on the east coast of Italy. Despite being in the middle of shifting bases, the 310th flew its largest single mission of the war on the 9th when almost 10,000 20-lb 'frag' bombs were dropped by 78 aircraft. The following 48 hours saw a further 220 B-25s sortied by the 310th BG.

The German High Command in Italy signed a ceasefire agreement in the Italian town of Caserta on 2 May 1945, and surrendered six days later. It was time for the 310th BG to go home.

The group had flown an astounding 989 missions since its combat debut in North Africa on 2 December 1942 – more than any other medium bomb group in the MTO! The 310th was deactivated on 12 September 1945 at Pomigliano, in Italy – its last base.

COMBAT VETERANS

Pilot 1Lt Bill Poole served with the 310th BG's 379th BS, completing 70 combat missions. He was trained to be a glider pilot, but wound up flying B-25s instead. Remembering how he felt during his first and later missions, Poole recounted;

'It was terrifying, no question about it. During my first and second missions we were shot at by 92 radar-controlled 88 mm cannons, those guns literally lighting up the sky right in front of us, their flak popping up all around us. I've got a piece of this flak in my archives. It came through the window behind by head and hit that big B-25 bulkhead right behind the pilot's deck. I was lucky enough to duck in time.

'Two men that I had known through most of my earlier training flew their first and last mission that same day. It was pure roulette as to who caught flak. Our aeroplanes routinely returned to base with hundreds of holes. We jokingly called it "flakto cumulus", as when you got close to it you'd start seeing orange centres, and before long you could smell it, and hear it, and not too long after that part of it would be raining on, or through, your aeroplane!

'My most memorable combat mission was number 69, flown on 9 April 1945. We were on a bomb run with our bomb-bay doors open. There were 300 aircraft, and everybody was dropping their bombs. The second box (another formation of B-25s at a higher altitude – Author) overtook us and dropped about 625 "daisy cutters", or "frag" bombs, through our formation. Eight of them hit my aeroplane. Luckily, only one had fallen far enough to arm itself, and it blew off the rearmost part of our left wing. One of them lodged in the left engine, but the others went right on through the aircraft – and I mean they *go right through*, making a hole the size of your head!

'We had no instrumentation as a result of this "friendly fire", and I still had to fly about 80 miles back to the airfield. The crew voted to fly back rather than jump. On the trip home we lost altitude all the way, despite still drawing full power. I kept telling the guys to go aft and find out what the hell the damage was, but no one could see it.

'When we approached the airfield, and after we had extended the landing gear, the crew saw long strings of rubber where the left main wheel was supposed to be. I told my co-pilot to give me about 15-20 degrees of flap. The aeroplane then started to turn itself upside down. "Put the flaps back up", I yelled!

'Knowing that the aeroplane was on the verge of a stall the whole time, I made a typical glider approach to the runway. The very second I started raising the nose, it quit flying – then we hit the ground. I couldn't hold it straight. I was having to carry full left engine and nothing on the right engine, and after about a quarter of the runway had passed by, I realised well, hell, I couldn't do that forever. I had to do something, so I asked my co-pilot, Milfried, to get ready to pull the landing gear back up. I told him, "When I say pull the gear up, pull the gear up!" I hollered the command, chopped the power and reached to shut off the master and two magneto switches. However, centrifugal force prevented me from doing that until the B-25 had stopped a skidding ground loop, with the gear collapsing sideways.

'The crew reported that our radio man, Jollie, was injured. We thought he was dead. I kept sending people back to check on him. "Hell, he's dead lieutenant, he's dead", they kept telling me!

'We had finally stopped and jumped the hell out the damn thing. The medics came running out and asked if anyone was hurt. "I think you've got a dead man in the back end of the aeroplane", I answered.

'We went down to see him that night in intensive care. "You can see him in the morning", we were told. Well, hell, in the morning he'd already been flown out. Yeah, we all thought he's been flown out all right, six feet under! But they never told you that sort of thing.

'In 1983, at a 57th BW convention held in Massachusetts, I found out that Jollie had indeed lived, but he'd lost a leg.

'For my final mission I got a new B-25J. We were required to do 70 missions by this late stage in the war, for the senior "brass" considered a mission to be less risky in 1945. So, on 19 April I reported to the briefing room. The target: Rovereto, in the Brenner Pass. I thought, "Oh my God, of all the damn places to have to go on my last mission".

'We were part of a flight of 24 aircraft (six B-25s in four layers, 300 to 500 ft above one another – Author) following another flight just like ours. Those aeroplanes were more than a mile ahead of us, and they were getting the hell shot out of them. You couldn't hear anything. You could only see the "flakto cumulus".

'My group didn't draw a single burst. I figured that they had used up all of their ammo on the first group, because that's the way it was in the waning days of the war.

'Prior to flying every single one of my 70 missions, I experienced apprehension that, in some ways, was worse than getting shot at. You would get so built up that all hell was going to break loose at any second that your feet got ice cold. In some of my earlier missions over the Brenner Pass in the dead of winter I'd have to open the side window because I'd be sweating like hell – but once again my feet were ice cold, as were my hands. Most of the time I had to sit on one hand and fly with the other.

A pair of 310th BG B-25Js unload four 1000-lb bombs apiece over the Brenner Pass in northern Italy. This area became the group's primary target in the final months of the war in Italy (USAF)

'The biggest impression that war left on me was that freedom doesn't come cheap. I cannot overemphasise that.'

1Lt (later Capt) Glenn T Black was a pilot with the 381st BS, and on his 56th mission he experienced an horrific episode in combat;

'On 21 June 1944 I had led a mission of 18 aircraft, successfully bombing a railroad viaduct at Piteccio Fabrica, in Italy. The next day most of our squadron was involved in a mission, but my crew and I, and a few others in our squadron, had the day off. However, we were told to remain in the squadron area, at least until 1700 hrs, because they might have a mission for us. It wasn't very long before 1700 hrs when we were called for a briefing. I was to take three aircraft from our squadron and three from the 380th and lead the third flight, which would in turn join up with 12 other B-25s from the 428th. The latter unit was leading the mission. Our target was to be a unique one!

'Personally, I didn't like the set-up, with 18 aircraft (three boxes of six) coming from three different squadrons. I felt we did a better job when all 18 were from the same squadron, but obviously that couldn't always be arranged.

'Allied ground troops were moving northward along the boot of Italy. Compared to the stalemate at Anzio, the present northward movement was rapid. It appeared that Allied forces would soon take Leghorn harbour. Intelligence reported that the Germans had plans to render this facility totally useless before retreating north. The report stated that they intended to take two floating hulks (ships or barges) and sink them across the two entrances to the harbour. The Allies would then be unable to bring in naval or merchant ships until the harbour entrances were cleared. Our mission was to sink those hulks right where they were, thus preventing the Germans from moving them into position in the harbour mouths.

'We weren't supposed to have a fighter escort on this mission, perhaps because our target didn't require us to be over Italy for very long. However, we picked up an escort – RAF Mustangs – at about the time we left the northern end of Corsica.

'We soon experienced the problem of a higher flight overrunning a lower one. Normally, we maintained an indicated airspeed (IAS) of 200 mph on our bomb runs, regardless of the altitude. Under standard conditions, including a standard lapse rate, true airspeed (TAS) is two per cent higher than IAS for each 1000 ft of altitude. At 8000 ft TAS would be 16 per cent higher than IAS. At 10,000 ft it would be 20 per cent higher, and at 12,000 ft 24 per cent higher. At 8000 ft at 200 mph IAS the TAS would be 223 mph, at 10,000 ft it would be 240 mph and at 12,000 ft it would be 248 mph. Those differences are not great, but it is obvious that the relative positions of our three six-aeroplane boxes were going to change. A higher flight may begin its bomb run behind a lower flight, but each second saw that distance diminish.

'Upon completion of my turn at the initial point (IP), we were well behind the other two flights.

'Normally, when attacking a coastal target, once bombs were away we would dive and turn toward the sea. The purpose of this manoeuvre was to get out of range of anti-aircraft fire as soon as possible. Of course the enemy gunners were aware of these things. It was my intention, this time, to do the opposite of the usual. Hoping to outwit the flak crews, I intended to climb and turn inland as soon as I heard "Bombs Away!"

'We tried to limit our bomb runs to three minutes or less – even one minute or less! Whatever the time may have been this day, it seemed to me that the bomb run was longer than usual. We had experienced an intercom malfunction the day before, and I began to wonder if we were having that problem again. Had Nick, our bombardier, released the bombs and called "bombs away", and I hadn't heard it? Flying in smooth air, the B-25 rose somewhat when 4000 lbs of bombs were released in about one second. Flak bursting close underneath or turbulent air gave the same feeling. I had not had any positive evidence that the bombs had been released, but I was tempted to assume they had been, and so I began my turn.

'Finally I did hear Nick's call, "Bombs Away!" By this time I was aware that the other two flights had turned toward the sea, and they were, I considered, too far ahead for us to catch them up. So, instead of climbing and turning inland as I had planned, I began a diving turn toward the sea.

'Moments later our aeroplane seemed to shudder and stop in mid-air. Everything turned brilliant white and time seemed to stop. Now I am aware that from bombs away to brilliant white occurred in just a matter of seconds. My right hand had been on the throttles. Now it was lying on my lap. Looking at my arm, I could see bone in the upper arm and bone in the lower arm. In between there was red meat that held the two parts together. My lower arm reminded me of an over-sized drumstick ready for the frying pan.

'Surveying the instrument panel, I realised that we had no power in our left engine. I called this to my co-pilot's attention, and Jerry feathered the prop – feathering a windmilling propeller reduces the drag. Reduced drag makes the aeroplane easier to control, and improves performance. Improving performance can make the difference between getting to a desired location and not making it that far.

War-weary B-25D-5 41-30105 returns to Fano at the end of yet another mission in mid 1944. This machine also lacks its ventral turret and nose guns, as well as yellow tail stripes (*Norm Taylor Collection*)

'The hydraulic pressure read zero, telling us that we could not lower the landing gear or flaps, or use the wheel brakes in a normal fashion. But aeroplanes have emergency procedures for such critical items. The bar in the artificial horizon that should have been horizontal, according to our present altitude, was vertical, but in day visual conditions that instrument was not essential for safe flight.

'When I wasn't concentrating on anything in particular, the pain became intense. I was now writhing in pain, turning my head to the right and left, fully each way, back and forth. Soon, either Grady Paul (the navigator) or Nick took hold of my head and held it against his chest. I don't know how long he held me, but I don't believe I repeated that head turning stuff after he released me. As I recall, not a word was said – but remember, verbal communication was exceedingly difficult in a B-25 during flight.

'One time when Jerry reached down between us, probably to make an adjustment to the rudder trim, his elbow bumped my arm in the wounded area above the shattered elbow. If my seat belt hadn't been fastened I expect I would have demonstrated how an ejection seat worked long before they were invented!

'As we approached Corsica, and before the island came in to sight, I began to become concerned about a different matter. As far as I knew Paul wasn't navigating, for he had been giving me first aid (sulphur powder, tourniquet, morphine etc.). We were above the clouds that had been there earlier when we were climbing out after take-off. Corsica's mountains reach up to about 8500 ft. I was concerned that we might let down between the clouds, but right into the mountains. Soon, however, we broke out below the clouds and could see the northern tip of the island still ahead of us.

'The northernmost fields were fighter fields, and their runways were shorter than ours – we wanted everything possible going in our favour. Additionally, these fields were either British or French, and we preferred to land at an American field. Furthermore, we knew there was an Army hospital not far from the 340th BG's base, which was about 30 miles closer than ours. Everything considered, the 340th base was the best place for us to land.

'Jerry radioed the 340th's tower, told them we had wounded aboard and obtained permission for a straight-in approach. When we were close enough to "emergency" lower the gear for landing, Jerry put the gear controls in the "down" position and I turned toward Paul in the navigator's compartment and signalled him to pump the gear down. In earlier B-25s a mechanical apparatus was used to lower the gear when the hydraulic system wasn't working. In the J-model, which we were in, a hydraulic "pump" system was used in such emergencies.

'Paul released the safety loop. The lever should have required quite an expenditure of muscle power to operate it. Paul could move it fully forward and back with his fingertips. Thus, the emergency gear system, just like the main system, was useless to us.

'At this time we were too low for anyone to bail out. With reduced power on the remaining engine, there was no assurance we could climb to altitude to allow bail out of any crewmember that might prefer that option. Compounding the danger of this impending crash-landing was

100-octane gasoline that was flooding the floor of the navigator's compartment. Whenever I looked back into that space I would be peering through a fog of gasoline fumes. Any kind of a spark from a radio or whatever could set off an explosion. What would a gear-up belly landing on a gravel runway produce in the way of sparks, and what about raw gas spilling onto the hot right engine?

'When Paul became aware that we were about to land with the gear up, he jettisoned the top hatch. Ordinarily, one enters and leaves a B-25 through hatches in the bottom of the fuselage. A gear-up belly landing would of course leave the aeroplane resting on the bottom of the fuselage, thus making these exits useless. A crash-landing could also twist the fuselage so badly that the top escape hatches would be jammed too, trapping crewmembers in a burning ship. Paul was correct to have jettisoned the top hatch.

'Before Paul started calling off airspeed, the last IAS I saw was 150 mph. We were then quite low, and only a few feet short of the runway. I let go of the yoke long enough to use my left hand to reduce the manifold pressure – the first time I recall the manifold pressure being reduced since we were hit. It's entirely possible that Jerry had reduced it without me being aware of it.

'As we flared out over the gravel runway I was quite conscious that because we had no landing gear extended underneath us, we would be lower (closer to the ground) when we contacted the runway. In the flare I felt Jerry holding backpressure on the elevator, keeping us higher than

Four 380th BS B-25J-1s approach their target in northern Italy in late 1944. The tightness of this formation may have been for the photographer's benefit only, as most attacks were carried out in a six-ship box formation (*NASM via Bob Haney*)

I wanted us to be. I was holding forward pressure, and I could see all too clearly that we were rapidly approaching the boulders that were at the far end of the runway. It was not my practice to yell at my crewmembers, but I wanted to be sure I was heard this time, and I yelled to Jerry, "Let's get this thing down!" Jerry relaxed the backpressure somewhat, and our tail touched down so smoothly that none of us remembered any jolt – none whatsoever. The last airspeed Paul called off was 135 mph. With no flaps and the single-engine configuration, we were probably not far from our stalling speed before touchdown – the speed at which lift is lost to the extent that the aeroplane drops.

'The possibility of catching fire or exploding was very great. Nock later related to me that his trousers were soaked with gasoline from their bottom to above his knees. The gas wasn't entirely that deep, but it was deep enough that like fuel soaks up into a lantern wick, the gas had soaked up to above his knees. And sometimes in a crash-landing fuel lines break and gas spills onto a hot engine, resulting in a fire and/or explosion. Our crew was very aware of these facts.

'Once we touched down there was no way in the world we could control the direction the aircraft was travelling. She'd literally have a mind of her own. Contacting the ground with our wings level, we had an advantage in the B-25 for the bottoms of the two engines were even with the bottom of the fuselage at that point. Thus, the engines served as outriggers. We were pointing straight down the runway when we touched down, and we slid straight ahead. As we were sliding down the runway, I reached with my left hand to turn off the master switch and the magneto switch to the right engine, and promptly got it stepped on – Paul had stepped onto the control pedestal (and my hand) to exit out the top hatch over the windshield!

'Everyone got out quickly and okay, except for Jerry – he was the last to leave because he helped me get out first.

'As Jerry and I were dealing with the parachute strap, I heard one of our crewmembers yell out to someone, "get out of here with that cigarette!" Although they were smokers, this was one time they drew the line quite forcibly. How ironic it would have been for us to survive the ordeal up to that point, only to have the aeroplane explode and burn because of someone coming toward us with a lighted cigarette!

'After I stepped out over the windshield I sat down on the nose. It was my intention to slide straight off the nose onto the ground, still holding my right hand with my left. Before I could do this, however, ambulance personnel who were already beside the nose told me to stay where I was until they could come alongside with a stretcher.

'Being anxious to distance myself from the possible explosion or fire, I didn't want to wait. I wanted to slide down as I had intended, but for some reason I did wait. Although I wasn't aware of being weak from the loss of blood, it's quite possible that I would have fallen flat on my face if I had slid off the nose. As it was, I didn't think there was any need for a stretcher, for I was confident I could have walked to the ambulance. But I did wait and lay down on the stretcher when they brought it alongside.

'The moment I was hit over Leghorn harbour I thought, "I should have become a minister". I don't look at this as indicating a special revelation from God. It's simply that if I had been preparing for the ministry I wouldn't have been over Italy at that time. Later, after the war, I did indeed become a minister.

'I was first pilot on all my missions. On my first mission, and on subsequent sea-sweep missions, I flew as element leader. On my first medium altitude missions I flew as a wingman, then as element leader, then flight leader. As a flight leader, I led the second 18 in two or three 36-aeroplane missions, and I led the entire group on at least two 18-aeroplane missions and one 24-aeroplane mission.

'When our squadron CO visited me in the hospital after I had been wounded, he apologised that he couldn't give me my promotion to captain because I hadn't been a first lieutenant long enough. I told him I didn't care, but afterwards I wished I had asked him to at least try, because I believe that what I had been doing merited it. After I was released from hospital and retired from the air force in 1946, I left with the rank of captain.'

S/Sgt George Underwood spent his tour of duty in the MTO sat in the top turret of a 381st BS Mitchell. He recalls;

'One mission from North Africa to the mainland of Italy called for 36 310th aircraft to bomb a key transportation centre near Naples. On the way to the target 50 enemy fighters intercepted and attempted to divert the six-aeroplane box formations, but it didn't work. The target – railroad-marshalling (switching) yards – was destroyed, and 18 of the attacking fighters were shot down. But the victory was costly to the 310th. Three of our aircraft were downed, and the remaining 33 B-25s returned to base riddled with flak shrapnel, cannon slugs and machine gun bullet holes. The mission earned the 310th one of its two Distinguished Unit Citations. Another thumbs up for victory.'

S/Sgt Underwood completed 68 combat missions over Italy from January to July 1944. He received four Air Medals, and feels that he was always the 'kid' of the crew, and that the 'older' guys had taken pretty good care of him. In his on-line biography (located at http://members.aol.com/famjustin/Underwoodbio.html), in part, he shares some of his more memorable experiences as follows;

'The top turret was designed to protect the B-25 and its crews from attacks from the upper hemisphere. The 0.50-cal machine guns rotated 360 degrees and swung from the horizontal to the vertical – zero degrees to 90 degrees. The field of fire and limits of the guns' movements in azimuth and in elevation were automatically controlled by cams and switches. The gunner could follow a target freely, firing as required without the bullets striking any part of the ship, or without the gun barrels bumping into any part of the fuselage.

'At the beginning of my tour I flew in a B-25G. I flew ten missions in the G-model, and they were the ones we had trained so long and hard for in Greenville, Texas, and Myrtle Beach, South Carolina. The first of our "G missions" were sea-sweeps along the coast of Italy over the Tyrrhenian Sea, and they were exciting. On these missions the

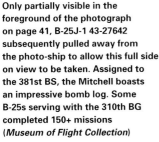

Only partially visible in the foreground of the photograph on page 41, B-25J-1 43-27642 subsequently pulled away from the photo-ship to allow this full side on view to be taken. Assigned to the 381st BS, the Mitchell boasts an impressive bomb log. Some B-25s serving with the 310th BG completed 150+ missions (*Museum of Flight Collection*)

entire crew could participate by shooting at sea-going vessels, aircraft and machine gun emplacements, and all at minimum flying altitude. Our propellers kicked up a mist of water spray as we buzzed the top of the sea on our anti-shipping raids. It seemed like the highest altitude we attained while on these sea-sweeps was when we returned to base, climbing all the way up to 500 ft to circle and land.

'One day our formation of four B-25Gs, flying in a straight line off Spiza, shot down a Dornier Do 24 three-engined flying boat which had been heading in the opposite direction to us at very low altitude – he was trying to hide from us in the seaspray. It was a big, slow, boxy and just plain ugly aeroplane, and it made a giant splash when it hit the water. With a bunch of eager gunners ahead of us already shooting at it, I didn't get much of a chance to fire at the Dormier.

'None of us claimed this "victory" since eight of us had fired at it. I thought about painting a one-eighth German cross on my turret since it was a confirmed "kill", but I thought better of it. We had got some flak on that mission but no fighters.

'The so-called E-boats were more difficult opponents. They were about the size of our navy's Patrol Torpedo (PT) boats, but they were moving flak platforms, mounting 20 mm, 40 mm and 88 mm cannon and machine guns. We hit many of them but sank none. They hit many of us but downed none. We broke even.

'Sea-sweeps often meant dawn patrols for us. Up at 0330 hrs, we climbed onto the backs of $2^1/2$ ton 6x6 trucks and were driven to the flightline, and our hardstand. Once at our aeroplane, we pulled the props around four or five times to get the oil that settled in the lower half of the piston cylinders equalised, pre-flighted it, warmed up the engines and got ready to go. Bomb loads were checked, and I made sure as armourer/gunner that the 0.50-cal machine gun belts and cans were full, and that we had a full load of 75 mm cannon rounds for our three-inch nose cannon.

'Those 75 mm cannon rounds were 26 inches long and weighed some 20 lbs each. Just above the cannon breech was a rack that held 20 rounds. We carried mostly high explosive warhead rounds, with a few armour-piercing shells thrown in for good measure just in case we met one or more of the dreaded German destroyers prevalent in the area. The cannon breech and ammunition rack was just aft, but quite a bit lower than the pilot's seat. That cannon could fire as fast as it could be loaded, and would toss rounds some miles distant, but usually in sea-sweeps 2000 yards was the maximum range.

'The cannon was a standard M4, with a specially-constructed spring to absorb some of its recoil shock. The barrel extended forward under the left side of the cockpit through the tunnel formerly used by the bombardier to reach his nose position. The muzzle of the cannon emerged from a concave port on the left side of the nose.

'We also flew B-25Hs. Both the G- and H-models were "cannon toting", and in addition to this weapon, they could also carry 3000 lbs of bombs for "skip bombing" and up to 18 0.50-cal machine guns for strafing and defence. The main difference between the G and the H was the location of the top turret, and that the former was built in Kansas City, Kansas, and the latter in Inglewood, California.

'My Bendix-built top turret was located on top of the aircraft. Its twin 0.50-cal machine guns were mounted on either side of my shoulders, and the ammunition containers mounted on the turret, each one holding 440 rounds of 0.50-cal ammo – enough for only a few seconds of continuous firing. I sat on a folding bicycle seat, and operated the electrically-powered turret with my hands via hand grips upon which were controls for regular speed, fast speed, intercom and the trigger, which fired the twin "fifties" simultaneously. The gunsight was optical and lighted. While I was up in the turret, both it and my head were constantly rotating, looking for the enemy.

'In the B-25G the top turret was mounted farther aft. We trained on the newer B-25H that had its top turret "up front", just behind the pilots. It was much more comfortable there than "in the back".

'My first mission (in a B-25G) was on 30 January 1944. From our base at Ghisonaccia, on Corsica, it took only 15-20 minutes to get to our target area. We had an escort of four Bell P-39 Airacobras from a nearby fighter base. The weather was good, and as we cruised along the Italian coast we spotted a German E-boat. It was loaded with ack-ack guns, and our formation engaged it. Our aircraft fired twice with the 75 mm cannon and registered a hit on it.

'Flying in single file formation on another mission, we flew down and between rows of houses in Leghorn harbour after spotting some ships tied up at the docks, with German gunners shooting at us from the windows of the houses. We shot back at them as we flew by. We were flying at about 200-225 mph, so shooting had to be done quickly, but it seemed like slow motion to me.

'Most of our bombing missions were flown at medium altitude – I didn't like them at all. We got lots of flak bombing from 10,000 ft, in 10°C temperature weather. On one mission we bombed off the lead ship – a B-25C – which had a bombardier. Our B-25G, of course, had no bombardier, so when the lead ship opened its bomb-bay doors so did we, and when he dropped his eight 500-lb bombs we did too. That's the way it was for medium altitude bombing, at least until we got into newer models (B-25Js) later in 1944.

'The most pleasant words spoken, and heard, in our earphones during a medium altitude (9000 to 12,000 ft) bombing mission were "bombs away". At that point the aeroplane gently lifted up after the bombs were released, and we could resume our evasive action, which was most often a sharp diving turn away from the target area, and all that flak. Bomb runs were very stressful. That was when the flak was at its heaviest, and the fighters would attack. We had to fly straight and level during the bombs runs.

'Bomb loads varied with the mission, and its objectives. We

380th BS B-25J-1 43-27575 *SKONK CHASER* accompanies three other Mitchells at relatively low altitude over central Italy in late 1944 (*J Sutay via Bob Haney*)

carried six 500-lb bombs during our sea-sweeps so as to allow us to "skip-bomb" any enemy vessels we found. Other mission loads included eight 250-lb bombs, three 1000-lb bombs, eight 500-lb bombs, clusters of "frag" bombs and, on a couple of missions, chaff, which took the form of aluminium foil strips that were dropped near the target to confuse the radar-controlled AA artillery guns that were firing at us. There's one other item in reference to the bombs.

A close up of the nose art that adorned 380th BS B-25J-1 43-27575 *SKONK CHASER*, which is also seen on page 45. The personalisation of aeroplanes by their air- and ground-crews was but a minor relief for the war-weary combat veterans of the USAAF in the MTO (*M George via Bob Haney*)

We never heard our bombs explode when they impacted. Unlike in the movies and the documentaries, where you are able to hear the bombs whistle and explode as the formations leave the target area, it just didn't happen in reality. We heard flak explode, but only when it was very, very close!

'After taking off for a medium altitude bombing mission, we would gather in our boxes of six aircraft, then into squadrons and finally into group formation, while all the time gaining the required altitude for the mission. The formations would gently move up and down in the air currents until the Initial Point (IP) was reached, from where we made the final run to our specified target.

'All gunners were very cautious when large, towering cloud formations were nearby, knowing full well that enemy fighters liked to hide in those clouds and bounce us from behind them. At the IP the most violent evasive action would take place. When in formation – wing tips to waist gunners' windows – our aircraft would move up and down and from side to side as we tried to put the German flak gunners off their aim.

'As previously mentioned, when we reached the target and started our bomb run, we would have to fly straight and level so that the bombardier could accurately drop our bomb loads. That meant we could not take any evasive action whatsoever.

'Our escort fighters would often be right there with us in the flak. It was an amazing show of courage on their part since they didn't have to be there at all. On one of our missions, a group of these fighters had been flying escort for some "heavies". Those B-17s and B-24s had very long bomb runs of several minutes, but we didn't. Having quickly lined up and dropped our bombs, we made our diving turn away and headed for home, leaving our fighter escorts in the target area catching the flak. Realising we had gone, the fighters peeled off and soon caught up with us!

'Our crew "volunteered" for a "nickling" (chaff-dropping) mission or two, the foil strips floating down toward the ground and confusing the radar sights that the German 88 mm cannons used. The "nickling" mission aeroplane usually flew alone, but near a formation, and it would drop its chaff in an effort to protect the bomber formation while over the target.

'There were a couple of missions that were really "rough", as we used to say. My 16th combat sortie was a medium altitude mission in which we bombed from 9500 ft. The target was Piombino harbour. We had 36 aircraft up, with 20 RAF Spitfires as our escorts, and we were carrying a "normal" bomb load of six 500-lb bombs. The date was 14 March 1944, and as usual the flak was both intense and accurate.

'Our squadron lost two ships over the target, and we barely made it back to Corsica, where we counted 82 holes in our B-25. We had also lost one of our engines, forcing us to make a wheels-up belly landing. The pilot did a great job, and smoothly crash-landed in spite of the bomber's battle-damaged state. Grass, rocks, dirt and dust were thrown up through the crawl-way as we skidded across the ground alongside the metal-covered runway.

'We didn't get our first J-model Mitchell until May 1944 – a beautiful, brand new, shiny silver machine (B-25J-1 43-27507). As an aside, on her first mission, she encountered some Axis fighters but they didn't bother her because the covering Spitfires bothered them.

'Only one other mission was as memorable as my 16th, and again it involved yet another crash-landing. That was my 58th mission, on 22 June 1944, over Leghorn harbour. Again, we had been shot up pretty bad over the target.

'Hit hard by flak, we limped back across the sea to Ghisonnacia on one engine, the other having been feathered. The good engine was spewing oil and smoke into the sky while we tiptoed toward home. We made it to the airfield and had to pump the wheels down. The hydraulic system had been shot out, yet we landed normally, not knowing that our nose wheel had also been damaged.

'The main gear "chirped" on the pierced metal runway, and as we slowed down enough to settle on the nose wheel, it collapsed with a loud, hard thumping noise. After we stopped, the nose was buried in the runway and our tail was sky high. We counted over 100 flak holes and one 88 mm hole through our left wing (which meant that the round had passed through the aeroplane without exploding), but no one was hurt.'

During its time in the MTO and ETO from late 1942 to late 1945, the 310th accomplished the following feats – 989 combat missions flown, totalling 57,244 combat hours and covering more than 6,298,555 miles; 1998 75 mm cannon rounds fired; 23,984 tons of bombs dropped; 121 enemy aircraft destroyed, not including 23 probably destroyed or 25 probably damaged; 208 enemy aircraft destroyed on the ground; and 206 enemy ships sunk, totalling an estimated 173,000 tons, not including probable or damaged shipping.

In return, the 310th BG had 493 personnel killed or injured in combat and 87 B-25s destroyed.

SKONK CHASER (in the background) formates with fellow 380th BS B-25J-15 44-28942 in late 1944. The latter machine featured no name or nose art (*J Sutay via Bob Haney*)

319th BG (Medium)

The 319th BG (M) consisted of the 437th, 438th, 439th and 440th BSs. And like the other B-25-equipped groups in the MTO, it ultimately came under the command of the 57th BW, Twelfth Air Force. It was, however, briefly assigned to the 42nd BW, Fifteenth Air Force (Heavy), from November 1943 to January 1944.

The 319th was constituted on 19 June 1942, activated one week later and inactivated on 18 December 1945. The group was based at Barksdale and Harding Fields, Louisiana; Shipdham and Horsham St Faith, England; St Leu, Tafaraoui, Maison Blanche and Telergma, Algeria; Oujda and Rabat Sale, French Morocco; Sedrata, Algeria; Djedeida, Tunisia; Sardinia; Corsica; Bradley Field, Connecticut; Columbia Army Air Base, South Carolina; Kadena and Machinato, Okinawa; and finally Fort Lewis, Washington. The 319th saw action in the EAME theatre, Algeria-French Morocco, Tunisia, Sicily, Naples-Foggia, Anzio, Rome-Arno, southern France, north Apennines, the Ryukyus and in the China offensive.

The group received two Distinguished Unit Citations, on 3 March 1944 for action over Rome and on 11 March 1944 for action over Florence. It also received the French *Croix de Guerre* with *Palmes* for its action in southern France during April-June 1944.

The 319th BG, nicknamed 'The Big Tail Birds', had originally trained with B-26 Marauders, and it arrived in the MTO between August and November 1942, via England. Operating from Arzeu beach, Algeria, it began combat operations in November 1942 during *Torch*, bombing targets in Tunisia until February 1943. On 10 November 1944 the 319th was reassigned to the 57th BW. It had formerly come under the jurisdiction of the 42nd BW.

The previous month, on 5 October, 319th BG CO Col Joseph R Hozapple announced that the group was going to convert to the B-25. In those days it usually took several months to swap aircraft types, but Col Hozapple told his men that the changeover would be made in just six weeks – without losing a single day of combat operations!

On 10 October the 319th got its first four B-25s for training purposes, and by the 16th each unit had four Mitchells apiece. Come 1 November, the 319th had enough bombers to go into combat. Three days later it used its new B-25s in anger – 'Same old targets, just a different aeroplane', commented T/Sgt Larry McCue, a tail gunner with the 437th BS.

Equipped with the B-25 for less than five months, the 319th BG is not particularly well served photographically during its brief spell on the Mitchell. This 438th B-25J-1 (43-27579) is seen unloading four 1000-lb bombs over the Brenner Pass in late 1944. All 319th BG B-25s had distinctive cobalt blue tails (*USAF*)

The crews had been flying their new B-25s for little more than a month when the 4 November mission was tasked. Now it was time to see what these new aeroplanes, and rookie Mitchell crews, could do.

The 319th flew four different missions against Italian targets on this day – a 24-aeroplane formation against the Piazzola rail bridge; a 16-ship formation against the rail bridge at Montebello; an 18-aeroplane raid on a bridge at Ponte S. Pietro Bergamo; and a 17-ship strike on the Orio Litta rail bridge. These missions were numbers 418-421 for the group. The bombs missed at Ponte S. Pietro Bergamo, but the other targets were heavily damaged. Ten days later Col Hozapple issued a letter of commendation to all group personnel. It read;

'I wish to extend my heartiest congratulations to all members of this command for the superb job done by you during our conversion from B-26 to B-25 type aircraft, and also during the initial phase of the new bomber's employment. The hard work and real co-operative spirit shown by everyone has again confirmed my belief that the 319th has no equal in this, or any other theatre. This is the first and only example known to me where a combat unit in the field has made a complete conversion without losing operational time. I am proud to be one of you.'

Not only had the challenge been met, it had been completed in record time. Of the remaining 26 days in November, the 319th sortied on 17 of them, completing 40 separate missions without any losses.

On 28 November the 319th flew its anniversary mission, commencing its third year of operations the following day. And despite December being a wet month, the group was able to fly 32 different missions in just 14 days, ranging as far afield as Pescheria, in Yugoslavia.

The 319th lost its first B-25 on 10 December over San Michele when a 439th BS machine went down in flames – only two parachutes were seen. Two more bombers were lost 12 days later, one falling near San Ambrosio and the other off the island of Capri. The crew of the latter bomber bailed out into the sea.

The group went back into action on 26 December, flying three missions with good results, and no losses. Three more missions were flown on the 31st, two to Chiusaforte and one to Piazzola. These completed mission numbers 490-492.

At 1600 hrs that same day, Col Hozapple called a meeting of all personnel. Standing on the flat bed of a 'Deuce-and-a-Half' truck, he announced that the 319th had flown its last mission in the MTO, and that it would be returning to the US. In January 1945, the 319th duly rotated back home, the group having been chosen to receive A-26 Invaders for use against the Japanese in the Pacific. Re-designated the 319th BG (Light), the group saw considerable action with the Douglas medium bomber between April and September 1945 as part of the Seventh Air Force, flying from bases on Okinawa.

Although the 319th BG (M) was only equipped with the B-25 for a relatively short period of time, the group nevertheless made a major contribution to the Allied victory in the MTO. Indeed, for two long and hard-fought months 'The Big Tail Birds' had attacked numerous targets in northern Italy and Yugoslavia with their Mitchells.

319th BG B-25Js return to Corsica from Italy in late 1944. A normal mission usually lasted anywhere from two-and-a-half to three-and-a-half hours. Endangering six crewmembers per aeroplane for such a long period of time in order to drop just a few relatively low-yield bombs seems to be a rather risky business when compared with today's 'smart' tactical bombing. However, during World War 2 this was state-of-the-art aerial warfare (*John Spoonamore via Bob Haney*)

COLOUR PLATES

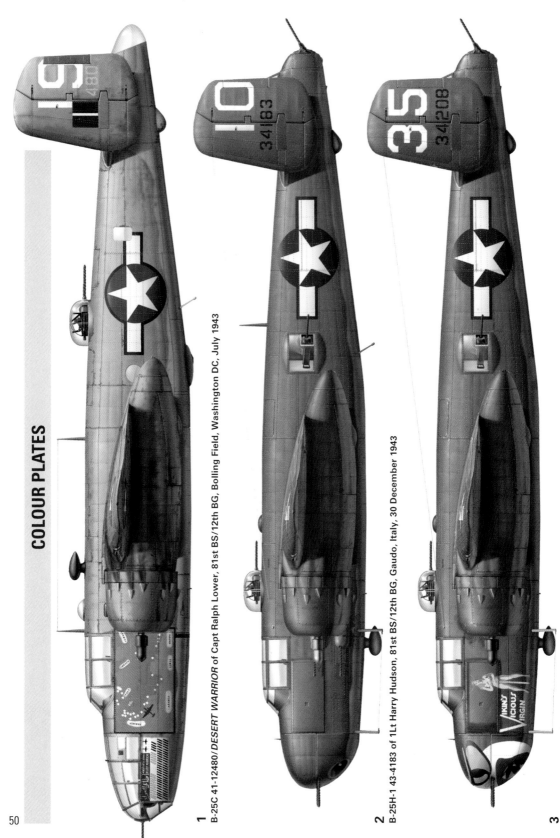

1
B-25C 41-12480/*DESERT WARRIOR* of Capt Ralph Lower, 81st BS/12th BG, Bolling Field, Washington DC, July 1943

2
B-25H-1 43-4183 of 1Lt Harry Hudson, 81st BS/12th BG, Gaudo, Italy, 30 December 1943

3
B-25H-1 43-4208/*VIKIN'S VICIOUS VIRGIN* of Capt Henry Vikin, 82nd BS/12th BG, Gaudo, Italy, 30 December 1943

4
B-25H-1 43-4381/*DOG DAIZE* of 1Lt Jared Miller, 82nd BS/12th BG, Gaudo, Italy, 28 December 1943

5
B-25C 41-12863 of Capt Doug Spawn, 82nd BS/12th BG, Tmed El Clel, Libya, 9 January 1943

6
B-25H-10 43-4909/*EATIN' KITTY* of 1Lt Charles Matheson, 82nd BS/12th BG, Foggia, Italy, 22 October 1943

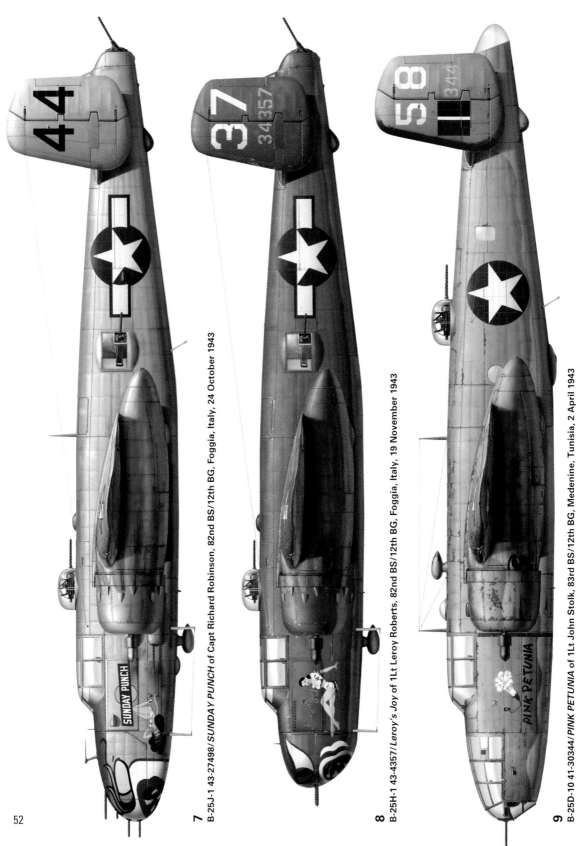

7
B-25J-1 43-27498/*SUNDAY PUNCH* of Capt Richard Robinson, 82nd BS/12th BG, Foggia, Italy, 24 October 1943

8
B-25H-1 43-4357/*Leroy's Joy* of 1Lt Leroy Roberts, 82nd BS/12th BG, Foggia, Italy, 19 November 1943

9
B-25D-10 41-30344/*PINK PETUNIA* of 1Lt John Stolk, 83rd BS/12th BG, Medenine, Tunisia, 2 April 1943

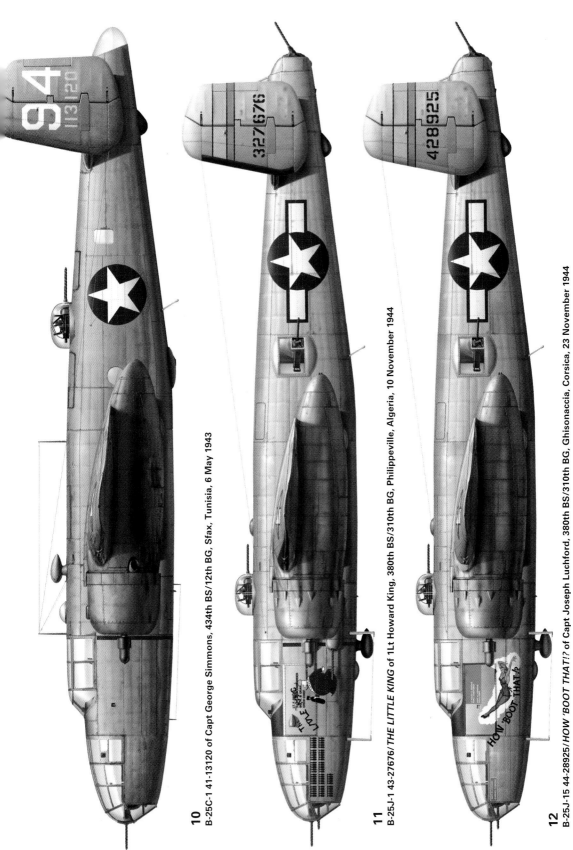

10
B-25C-1 41-13120 of Capt George Simmons, 434th BS/12th BG, Sfax, Tunisia, 6 May 1943

11
B-25J-1 43-27676/ *THE LITTLE KING* of 1Lt Howard King, 380th BS/310th BG, Philippeville, Algeria, 10 November 1944

12
B-25J-15 44-28925/*HOW 'BOOT THAT!?* of Capt Joseph Luchford, 380th BS/310th BG, Ghisonaccia, Corsica, 23 November 1944

13
B-25C-15 42-32505 of 2Lt William Wolfe, 381st BS/310th BG, Temime, Tunisia, 27 August 1943

14
B-25J-10 43-36099 of 1Lt John Marlow, 440th BS/319th BG, Djedeida, Tunisia, 7 July 1944

15
B-25J-1 43-27698 of Capt Henry Miller, 445th BS/321st BG, Falconara, Italy, 10 January 1945

16
B-25C-1 41-13207/ *OH-7* of 2Lt Charles Irwin, 445th BS/321st BG, Oujda, French Morocco, 14 February 1943

17
B-25J-1 43-27747/ *PEGGY LOU* of 1Lt Michael Murphy, 445th BS/321st BG, Soliman, Tunisia, 27 August 1943

18
B-25J-1 43-27475 of 1Lt Donald Nickelson, 447th BS/321st BG, Falconara, Italy, 11 November 1944

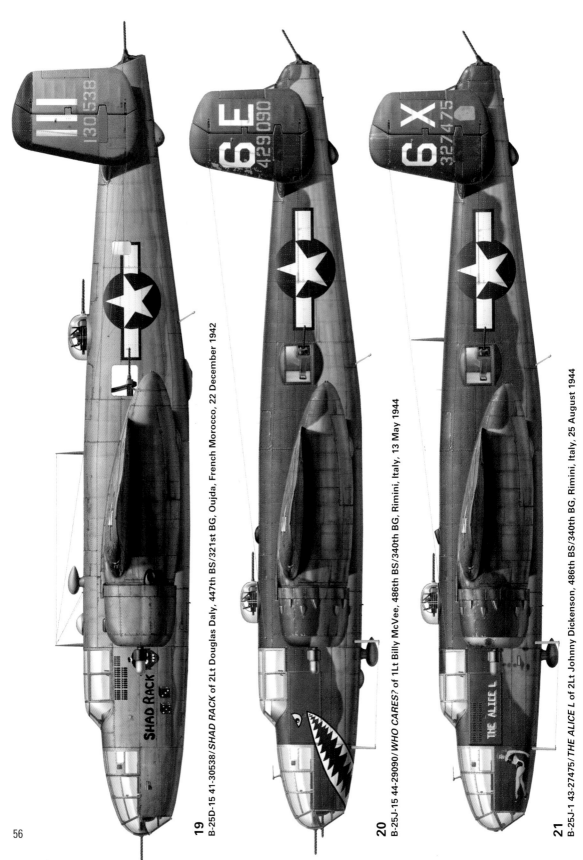

19
B-25D-15 41-30538/*SHAD RACK* of 2Lt Douglas Daly, 447th BS/321st BG, Oujda, French Morocco, 22 December 1942

20
B-25J-15 44-29090/*WHO CARES?* of 1Lt Billy McVee, 486th BS/340th BG, Rimini, Italy, 13 May 1944

21
B-25J-1 43-27475/*THE ALICE L* of 2Lt Johnny Dickenson, 486th BS/340th BG, Rimini, Italy, 25 August 1944

22
B-25J-5 43-27900/*BOTTOMS-UP II* of 1Lt Clarence Morton, 486th BS/340th BG, Gaudo, Italy, 12 March 1944

23
B-25C 41-12472 of 1Lt George Wamsley, 487th BS/340th BG, Landing Ground 99 (El Kabrit), Egypt, 12 December 1942

24
B-25J-1 43-4065/*G.I. JOES* of Capt Joseph P Turner, 487th BS/340th BG, Rimini, Italy, 24 July 1944

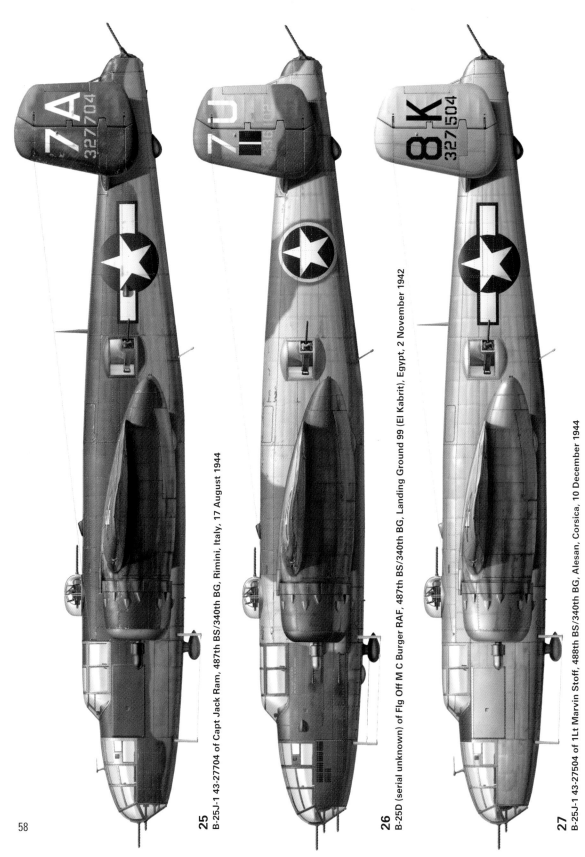

58

25
B-25J-1 43-27704 of Capt Jack Ram, 487th BS/340th BG, Rimini, Italy, 17 August 1944

26
B-25D (serial unknown) of Flg Off M C Burger RAF, 487th BS/340th BG, Landing Ground 99 (El Kabrit), Egypt, 2 November 1942

27
B-25J-1 43-27504 of 1Lt Marvin Stoff, 488th BS/340th BG, Alesan, Corsica, 10 December 1944

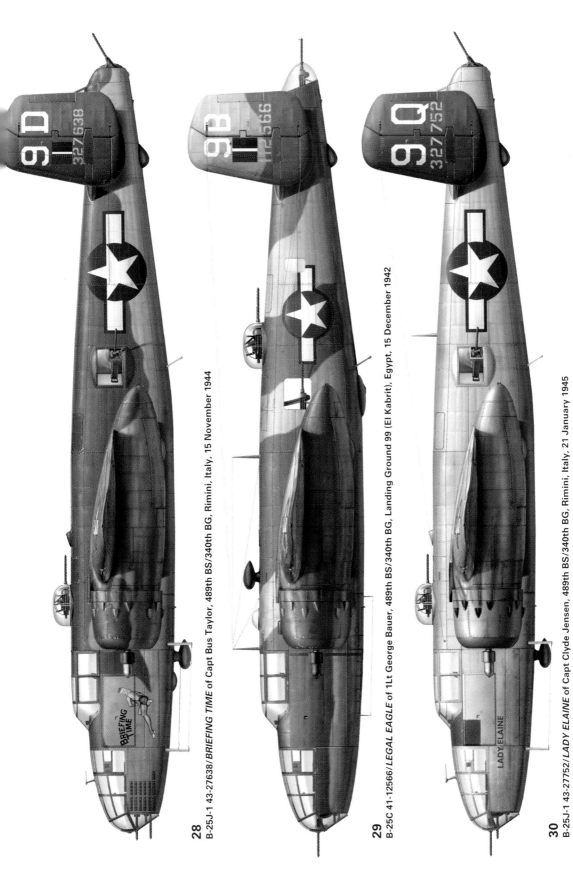

28
B-25J-1 43-27638/*BRIEFING TIME* of Capt Bus Taylor, 489th BS/340th BG, Rimini, Italy, 15 November 1944

29
B-25C 41-12566/*LEGAL EAGLE* of 1Lt George Bauer, 489th BS/340th BG, Landing Ground 99 (El Kabrit), Egypt, 15 December 1942

30
B-25J-1 43-27752/*LADY ELAINE* of Capt Clyde Jensen, 489th BS/340th BG, Rimini, Italy, 21 January 1945

This nose-art section has been specially created by profile artist Jim Laurier so as to better illustrate the colourful artworks worn by a number of the B-25s featured in profile. These ten drawings have been produced following exhaustive cross-referencing with published bomb group histories, correspondence with surviving veterans and the detailed study of original photographs.

1

2

3

4

5

6

7

8

9

10

11

321st BG (Medium)

The 321st BG (M) also fought throughout the MTO campaign with four medium bomb squadrons assigned to it, namely the 445th, 446th, 447th and 448th BSs. Constituted on 19 June 1942, and activated one week later, the group was inactivated on 12 September 1945. It saw action in the EAME theatre, Tunisia, Sicily, Naples-Foggia, Rome-Arno, southern France, north Apennines, central Europe and the Po River Valley. The group earned two Distinguished Unit Citations, the first over Athens on 3 October 1943 and the second in France on 18 August 1944.

Between June 1942 and August 1945, the 321st was stationed at Columbia Army Air Base and Walterboro, South Carolina; De Ridder Army Air Base, Louisiana; Ain M'lila, Algeria; Souk-el-Arba, Tunisia; Soliman, Tunisia; Solenzara, Corsica; and Grottaglie, Amendola, Vincenzo, Gaudo, Falconara and Pomigliano, Italy.

The 321st's first training phase had been conducted at Columbia, followed by a move to Walterboro for its second, and final, period of basic tuition. Once this training had been completed (including 'skip-bombing' practice at Eglin Field, Florida), the 321st was declared combat ready. But instead of immediately going overseas, it was called upon to participate in manoeuvres in Louisiana, where it flew low altitude support missions for tactical ground forces.

After taking part in this exercise, the 321st had its aircraft modified through the removal of their now ineffective (as had been already proven in combat) lower gun turrets. Additional 0.50-cal machine guns were installed in the waist and tail positions, and extra armour plating added in an effort to protect each and every crewmember.

The 321st arrived at Oujda, in French Morocco, on 2 March 1943, where it was assigned to the Twelfth Air Force. Commanded by Col Robert D Knapp, the group's ground and flight echelons met up at Oujda for the first time since they had separated at De Ridder on 21 January 1943. From De Ridder, the aircrew had gone to Brooks Field, Florida, while the groundcrews had been transported to New York City to board a troop ship for their trip across the Atlantic.

On Staten Island, the groundcrews boarded the USS *Elizabeth C Stanton* on 7 February. The ship departed at dawn the following day, and after a two-week trip as

These 321st machines are seen flying in a typical six-aeroplane box formation. Such a box would generally join up with two or three other similar-sized groups to make 18- to 24-aeroplane formations (*D Porter via J Hurley and Bob Haney*)

part of a 26-ship convoy (including escorts), the vessel docked safely at Oran on 21 February.

The aircrews departed Brooks Field, West Palm Beach, in 54 B-25C/D on 15 February 1943, thus beginning the first leg of their long overseas hop. Refuelling and maintenance was carried out in Puerto Rico, British Guiana, Belem and Natal, in Brazil, the Ascension Islands, Monrovia, Liberia, Dakar, French West Africa and Marrakech, before landing at Oujda on 2 March.

This crossing by the 321st marked a pioneering achievement, for it was the first time a bomb group had succeeded in making the southern route crossing in such large numbers without the loss of a single bomber. The 12th BG had previously made the crossing with 64 B-25s, again without loss, but not all at once – one formation of 32 aircraft had arrived one day, followed by another 24 hours later.

On 15 March 1943 the 321st made its combat debut. Flying from Ain M'lila, 15 B-25s took off to attack an airstrip at Mezzouna, in Tunisia. P-38s of the 57th FW escorted the formation, and although it encountered heavy flak, all of the bombers returned safely. The attack was directed at enemy aircraft around the base, and several strings of fragmentation bombs found their mark. When the B-25s turned for home a number of fires were seen to be burning all around the airstrip.

The group's first encounter with fighters occurred just five days later. The B-25s had sortied on a shipping sweep to the Sicilian Straits when about 30 fighters from bases in Tunisia bounced them. Seven fighters were claimed to have been destroyed, four of them falling to the modified gun positions. Tail gunners accounted for one Bf 109 and one Me 410, as did left-hand waist gunners. Top turret and nose gunners downed the remaining three fighters. One B-25 was shot down and another so badly damaged that it had to crash-land. Both of these bombers had been crippled by flak.

For its early combat operations, the 321st had been assigned to the 47th BW, which was then a part of Maj Gen Doolittle's North African Strategic Air Force.

By mid May 1943 the battle for Tunisia was over, and the Axis powers had lost their foothold in North Africa. By this time the 321st had flown 51 missions, 30 of which had been directed against shipping in the Sicilian Straits, 15 against airfields, four against the communications centre at Mateur, and single missions against harbour installations and a railway junction.

On 28 May the 321st put up a relatively large formation of 29 Mitchells to attack Bo Rizzo airfield on Sicily. During the mission, touted as highly successful, the Axis met the B-25s with some 30 to 50 fighters, including German Bf 109s, Fw 190s and Italian C.202s. Apparently, it did not matter that the 321st was outnumbered, because the enemy pilots seemed to be both inexperienced and unaware of the revised armament being carried by these B-25s. Moreover, with the additional 'fifties', the group's gunners were able to claim 17 enemy fighters shot down 'with the greatest of ease', according to a post-mission report. These proved to be 'duck gallery' shots, the report added.

The desperate, but aggressive, Axis fighter pilots had tried 'every trick in the book', including their newest – air-to-air bombing. Some of the fighters climbed about 1000 to 3000 ft above the B-25s to drop their bombs, which usually exploded below the formations. Despite these attacks, each and every one of the 29 Mitchells despatched returned safely to base. And the Bo Rizzo airfield suffered a great deal of damage, including the destruction of numerous aircraft in their revetments and dispersal areas.

Despite the assault of Sicily being well and truly underway, the small and heavily fortified islands of Pantelleria and Lampedusa, off the coast of Tunisia, were still held by enemy troops following the departure of Axis forces from North Africa. Both islands had harbours, and Pantelleria had an airfield, thus posing a threat to Allied ships and aircraft crossing the Mediterranean.

The neutralising of both islands would be entrusted to Allied air power. On 11 and 12 June, wave after wave of medium and heavy bombers (including B-25s of the 321st) attacked the islands, bombing gun emplacements, defensive installations, harbours and the airfield on Pantelleria. A large white cross on the latter site, and others openly displayed on both islands, signified the enemy's capitulation on the 13th.

On 21 June 36 B-25s from the 321st attacked Battipaglia, thus striking the first blow delivered on the Italian mainland. The mission was successfully completed without loss (without encountering any opposition whatsoever, in fact), yet Italian radio broadcast the erroneous statement that 26 Mitchells had been downed during the raid!

The 321st played its part in the invasion of Sicily on 10 July when B-25s attacked Axis troop concentrations and barracks at Palazzolo, followed later in the day by strikes against the large Trapani-Milo airfield in western Sicily. While no aircraft were lost, 19 sustained flak damage.

Nine days later an aerial armada of some 500 Allied aircraft struck suddenly and decisively at military targets in and around Rome, and B-25s from the 321st helped carry out this first attack on the Italian capital. With group CO Col Knapp in the lead Mitchell of a 72-aeroplane formation (the largest ever sortied by the group), the 321st hit the airfield at Ciampino – a strategic target utilised by a significant number of enemy fighters. Up to a dozen Axis fighters attacked the formation, but these were driven off by the bombers' gunners. One B-25 was shot down by flak, however, and another had to make an emergency landing at Biserte after suffering shrapnel damage.

In late July the 321st began to receive Inglewood-built G-model B-25s, and on 5 August four of these machines attacked a railway-switching yard at Guspini, on the island of Sardinia. As previously mentioned, the B-25G featured a large nose-mounted 75 mm cannon, and during the strike the four aircraft fired 36 rounds, scoring a number of direct hits that set the yard alight. The bombers had come in at an

B-25C-1 41-13207 *OH-7* flew with the 445th BS during the first months of the 321st BG's service in the MTO. The bomber is seen here surrounded by empty ammunition boxes at Ain M'lila airfield in Algeria. Note the wrecked hangar behind the B-25. *OH-7* was later written off in a belly landing on 14 February 1943, its hydraulic system having been wrecked by flak during an attack on Axis shipping off Libya (*Clyde Turner via Bob Haney*)

altitude of just 300 ft, encountering no opposition whatsoever.

T/Sgt John Jarvis, a radioman with the 445th BS, had this to say about the B-25G;

'It's been claimed that some 75 mm cannoneers were able to get off three or four rounds in one pass. During strafing runs against Axis shipping, or anything else for that matter, the men who loaded the cannons on B-25Gs had to be incredibly fast to accomplish that feat. Getting off three or four rounds of 75 mm artillery during one pass would have been very good indeed. I was never in an attack at sea, but against Panzers it was rare that we got off two rounds. But one round usually did the trick, with pieces of the tank flying high into the air. When shaped-charge shells like those 75 mm brutes we used hit a tank, it blew it up from the inside out. Going up against AA artillery from a ship was hairy, and I certainly respect those crews that did it. It took guts. But I'm not sure of those three to four rounds per pass claims.

'I flew 38 missions (the USAAF said 39, but that's wrong) and some of those were "milk runs". But we did at times go right into the face of heavy fire and, sadly, we lost a lot of aeroplanes and their crews. It is a tribute to the design of the nimble B-25 that we didn't lose more, for it could take evasive action (of a sort) even when attacking. Of the B-25 itself (all versions), it was a marvellous aeroplane in the hands of a good, strong pilot. I say strong, because there was no hydraulic boost on the flight controls.

'My pilot was a Maj Vaughn, who was excellent. But he was 35 years old at the time, and we thought of him as an old man! When I think back about that now as I near my 81st birthday, I have to smile. He was a quiet man, and we knew he wouldn't ever do anything nutty – like the one goofy pilot who left the formation and took off after an Me 109 as if his B-25 was a fighter (of course he didn't get it).'

After five weeks of fighting, Sicily fell to the Allies on 17 August 1943. Crews from the 321st had played an active part in the campaign, flying their B-25s against a wide variety of targets in 56 missions, and completing more than 2000 sorties.

One B-25 bombardier with the 321st BG was Capt Richard E Krause of the 445th BS. He flew 70 combat missions between April 1944 and May 1945, and here he recalls his most memorable mission;

'It was 18 August 1944, when our group attacked the enemy ships at Toulon Harbour in southern France. The harbour was ringed with a heavy net of anti-aircraft guns and, for that reason, was always designated as a "heavy" bomber target, since they attacked from higher altitude where they wouldn't be so vulnerable to the intense flak. To send "medium" bombers over that target was generally considered out of the question. No less than 82 heavy anti-aircraft guns protected the

Dubbed the *Shit House Mouse* by its crew, and adorned with suitably descriptive nose art, B-25J-1 43-27716 of the 445th BS had completed 45 missions by the time this photograph was taken in 1944. Each mission was marked with a mouse symbol. Some of these sorties had seen the crew employing the newly-introduced, radar-assisted, bombing through overcast (BTO) system. This equipment allowed crews to accurately hit their targets despite the latter being obscured by dense cloud – often a problem in the MTO (*Richard Krause*)

harbour, and it seemed that all of them had opened up on our B-25s. The primary target of the attack was the 702 ft-long Vichy French battleship *Strasbourg*, and alongside her a cruiser in the *La Galissonniere* class, plus a submarine. The heavy flak barrage damaged 27 of the group's bombers, but all returned from the mission safely.

'When our B-25s approached the target area at a typical medium bomber altitude of 10,000 ft, we immediately spotted the battleship, cruiser and submarine. The German anti-aircraft gunners greeted us with a heavy barrage-type flak pattern through which our bombers had to fly to reach the target.

'The outstanding results of the attack represented one of the heaviest blows ever struck at Axis shipping in the Mediterranean. The submarine was sunk, the cruiser keeled over on its side and the battleship was gutted by fire and completely disabled. Our group received the Presidential Citation for this attack. Twelfth Air Force called the raid "one of the most destructive ever carried out by a group of medium bombers".'

1Lt Edward V 'Ed' Crinnion of the 446th BS/321st BG flew 67 combat missions between 1 September 1944 and 1 April 1945 – 28 as co-pilot and 39 as first pilot. He was awarded a DFC and an Air Medal with seven Oak Leaf Clusters. Of his tour he related;

'On my first mission not all four 1000-lb bombs on board released over the target. One became hung up in the bomb-bay, partially loosened from its mount. The crew tried to drop it into the Mediterranean Sea, but the bombardier could not dislodge it. As we landed at Solenzara, on Corsica, the bomb dropped to the runway and tore a gash in the bottom of the fuselage from the aft end of the bomb-bay to the tail. Fortunately, the arming mechanism on the nose of the bomb had not rotated enough to activate the device.

'On my second mission flak penetrated the floor of the cockpit, passing between me and the first pilot, before exiting through the top of the canopy. Another burst shattered the instrument panel. Without instruments – especially an air speed indicator – landing was difficult. Back at Solenzara, the pilot of another B-25 was notified of our problem, and he positioned his aeroplane in such a way that my bomber could flying on his wing and execute a safe landing. The guide aeroplane made an ordinary approach, slightly to the left of the runway, and we flew on his right wing. As we landed, the guide pilot "poured on the coal" and circled for his own landing procedure.

'I thought to myself, "two missions down, only 68 more to go. Yikes!" It was status quo for us medium bomber types to fly 70 missions before we could go home.

'Finally, after 28 missions as a co-pilot, I was assigned my own aeroplane (a B-25J) and crew on 4 December 1944. The previous commander of the bomber had been 1Lt Russell V Grove. His wife was enlisted in the US Navy, so he had named his aeroplane *LI'L ADMIRAL*. The nose art was a drawing of a beautiful girl in a bathing suit. I had a sweetheart at home by the name of Jane, who I later married. I eventually renamed my aeroplane *LADY JANE*.

'On any particular mission, each one of the four squadrons within the 321st BG mounted its own formation of nine or twelve aeroplanes

Lt Voelker of the 445th BS climbs out of the forward entry/exit hatch, with open bomb-bay doors behind him (*Richard Krause*)

The 445th BS's Lt Richard Krause poses with B-25J *Cuddle Bunny* on Corsica in early 1944. His 'main ride' was on the *Shit House Mouse* (*Richard Krause*)

in elements of three. The bombing altitude usually ranged from 9000 to 13,000 ft in 500-ft increments. The bomb run – the time from the IP to the point of release – usually took about four minutes. This was four minutes of hell, as everyone in the formation was a sitting duck, flying straight and level, unable to take any evasive action.

'On my 42nd, 43rd and 44th missions, I was most fortunate to get back to base. This was especially true of my 42nd mission. As it happened, on 13 February 1945 my aeroplane suffered very unusual damage. Flak had made my right servo tab (which operated the rudder) useless. The broken tab began to oscillate, causing the right rudder to move in unison. Since the controls to the dual rudders were linked, the left rudder moved in harmony with the right rudder.

'As I neared Allied territory, I broke away from the rest of the formation and headed for my first emergency landing at a friendly field, which I found just over the frontline. Even with the rudders literally "flapping in the breeze", it proved to be a very smooth landing.

'My 67th mission proved to be my last. I'd been grounded. It was 1 April 1945 – Easter Sunday – and I immediately wrote a letter home:

'"Dear folks,

'"I haven't much time so this will be just a note to wish everyone a Happy Easter, and to tell you some really good news.

'"This is an Easter Sunday I'll never forget. Today I flew my 67th mission, and when I returned I found that it was my last. I'm grounded for combat and free to go home as soon as my orders are ready, which will probably be in about three or four weeks. Boy! What a feeling to know you'll be going home in a few weeks. 'Finis la Guerre'.

'"It's 3:45 pm, and I want to go to mass at 4:00 pm, so I'll get this in the mail. I want you to know as soon as possible. There'll be a letter following soon.

'"Love to all,

'"Ed"'

'Under orders from Capt J E Warren, squadron surgeon, I was grounded, and recommended for rotation back to the states. The doc, in part, wrote;

'"Lt Crinnion flew 28 missions as co-pilot and 39 as first pilot. His manner and performance has been excellent. He has encountered more hazards than the average crewman. The controls of his aeroplane were damaged by flak on his 42nd, 43rd and 44th missions. On his 45th mission a tyre was punctured by flak, making an emergency landing necessary at his home base. On his 60th mission the aeroplane directly behind him was shot down and his aeroplane received 80+ flak holes. These events combined have greatly increased his fear in the air. Apprehension has now begun to interfere with efficiency. Insomnia, battle dreams, restlessness and weight loss have become permanent symptoms. Adequate rest has failed to alleviate his symptoms. I recommended that 1Lt Crinnion be returned to the Zone of the Interior for rehabilitation and reassignment."'

'With that, and my ensuing orders, I got to go home.'

The late S/Sgt Brendon J Murphy was a Radio Operator/Gunner with the 445th BS. He flew 24 missions from 17 March to 25 April 1945. His daughter, Amy Murphy Demeo, remembers:

On 22 March 1944 Mt Vesuvius erupted, spewing a huge cloud of hot volcanic ash and brimstone into the air. When this came back to earth, it blanketed a number of Allied airfields in the vicinity of Naples. This 321st BG machine, its canvas covers hastily draped over its forward fuselage and engines, seemingly cowers beneath the massive volcanic cloud. The group had a considerable number of its Mitchells written off in the aftermath of the eruption (*D Mershon via Bob Haney*)

'My father was trained as a Radio Operator, which means he knew how to covertly contact home base, and be able to switch signals using high frequency channels – not an easy task. In this way the aircraft could maintain radio silence in order to keep the Germans from tracking the squadron's position as it proceeded to the target. In addition, he was trained as a 0.50-cal machine gun Gunner.

'When he was not operating the radio, he would fire one of the "fifties" from a waist window. In emergencies, he also served as a Top Turret Gunner. The B-25 was heavily armed, and enemy fighters avoided it when it wasn't on a bomb run because it could bring ten "fifties" per aeroplane to bear, and the B-25s flew very, very close to each other, making for even more heavily concentrated firepower.'

T/Sgt Isidore Ifshin was a Flight Engineer/Top Turret Gunner in the 447th BS, and he flew 60 combat missions. One of his missions was described by fellow crewman T/Sgt Ben Guild in an article entitled 'A Mission to Remember', which was published in an issue of the 57th BW Association journal *The Bridgebusters*. It is reproduced here with the permission of Isidore Ifshin;

'Unknown to us in the 447th, the war was supposedly winding down in December 1944. The 321st was hitting the Po River Valley pretty hard on a regular basis. While the German fighter cover was more lax than the previous year, the flak was just as heavy around most targets, and just as accurate.

'I had flown a mission on 5 December, which although not exactly a "milk run", wasn't too hot either. My memory is a bit foggy after all this time. I don't remember much about the previous 56 missions I flew, or the targets we hit, or even whether they were "hot" or not. But I sure remember my 57th mission.

'I had sacked out the previous night thinking how nice it was that I didn't have to fly for a couple of days. But that was not to be. You see, I was one of those so-called Lead Radio Operator/Gunner people in the 447th, and we took turns taking this duty.

'At dawn on 6 December, a runner from group headquarters came into my tent and woke everybody up trying to find me. There were six ticked off guys right then, but not as ticked off as I was. The runner told me that a staff sergeant

The six-man crew of the 445th BS's B-25C *POOPSIE* pose for the camera, along with the aircraft's crew chief and the real 'Poopsie'! The canine theme has even been carried over to the bomber's mission tally (*Fred Hayner Collection*)

A cluster of 20-lb anti-personnel 'frag' bombs fall away from B-25J-1 43-27698 *PEGGY LOU* of the 445th BS during a mission over Italy in 1944. The aircraft flying abreast of it, B-25J-1 43-27748, released its volley of 'frag' bombs seconds later (*Museum of Flight Collection*)

Boasting an impressive mission tallyboard beneath its cockpit, this 446th BS B-25J is seen departing its base in October 1944 at the start of yet another sortie against targets in the Po River Valley. Axis bridges and railway lines in this strategically important area of northern Italy were literally ripped apart by continuous medium bomber sorties (*Norm Taylor Collection*)

447th BS B-25J-10 43-27475/'111' was flown by Donald Nickelson from Falconara, in Italy, during the autumn of 1944. On 11 November Nickelson and his machine were part of an 18-aeroplane formation, split into three six-bomber boxes, that dropped 'frag' bombs on Axis troop convoys attempting to move through the Brenner Pass. The group suffered no losses, but a single B-25J from the 447th had about 60 per cent of its right vertical tail and rudder blown off. However, the rugged Mitchell was coaxed home with only a single working rudder (*via Gary Farrar*)

who had recently come back from leave in Naples had come down with a social disease (you know what I mean) that left him unfit to fly, so I had to take his place.

'As I hurriedly dressed for flying, I suddenly got a real funny feeling – sort of a premonition of things to come. I put all my personal belongings into my foot locker, and told the guys that if I didn't come back to please send all my things home to my mother. They just laughed like they always did when something like that came up. We all thought that only people from others tents were lost, right?

'We were to bomb the heavily-defended railway marshalling yards at Rovereto, which fed the Brenner Pass rail line. When I found out what the target was, I told the recuperating staff sergeant that he owed me one, and that if I didn't come back I'd haunt him for the rest of his life.

'I hadn't flown with that particular crew before. The pilot was Lt Remmel and his co-pilot Lt Speer. I don't remember the names of the navigator or the bombardier, except that one of them was Lt Darrel. The engineer was T/Sgt Ifshin and a Sgt Barratt was our tail gunner. It was an experienced crew, with numerous missions under their belts.

'The aeroplane was a B-25J, but I don't remember the name she carried. Our ship, and 15 others, were loaded with eight 500-lb bombs. When we hit the target area we were flying at 11,200 ft.

'The flight went well until we were into the bomb run – we didn't get a chance to drop our bombs. The flak was suddenly thick and heavy and we got hit. The left engine took a direct hit and it fell out of the nacelle. We were then on fire!

'Remmel screamed "BAIL OUT!, BAIL OUT!", and bail out we did. He didn't have to tell us twice. Barratt and I got out the rear hatch but I

don't know how the bombardier, top turret gunner and navigator got out. The pilots did not escape, however, for they sacrificed their lives flying an unflyable aeroplane, holding it steady long enough for five guys to get out. They will never be forgotten.

'We were so low over the mountains that my parachute only swung twice before I found myself in the deep snow of the Italian Alps. I was rescued, and wound up in a little village called Mori with the other four survivors. I was told later that the aeroplane hadn't flown another 200 ft before it exploded into a giant fireball.'

340th BG (Medium)

Just like the aforementioned medium bomb groups featured in this volume, the 340th BG (M) also controlled a quartet of medium bomb squadrons – the 486th, 487th, 488th and 489th BSs.

The 340th was constituted on 10 August 1942 and activated ten days later. Its saw action in the EAME theatre, Tunisia, Sicily, Naples-Foggia, Anzio, Rome-Arno, southern France, north Apennines, central Europe and the Po River Valley. The group's awards and citations included a Distinguished Unit Citation (DUC) for its performance in North Africa and Sicily between April and 17 August 1943, and a second DUC for its action over Italy on 23 September 1944.

The group operated from Columbia Army Air Base and Walterboro, South Carolina; El Kabrit, Egypt; Medenine, Sfax and Hergia, Tunisia; Comiso and Catania, Sicily; San Pancrazio, Foggia, Pompeii, Paestum and Rimini, Italy; Corsica; Seymour Johnson Field, North Carolina; before finally returning to Columbia Army Air Base.

The 340th BG arrived in the MTO, at El Kabrit, in March 1943. It was first assigned to the Ninth Air Force, and then moved to the Twelfth in August 1943. Its two-year combat tenure ran from

Ordnance men from the 340th BG prepare 'frag' bomb clusters for an anti-personnel bombing mission. Each fragmentation bomb weighed 20 lbs (*J Pecora via Bob Haney*)

A German-held airfield in Italy is plastered by 486th BS 'frag' bombs, dropped from 10,000 ft. Prime targets for Allied medium bombers in the MTO included airfields (and the aeroplanes on them), bridges, roads, railway lines and marshalling yards (*Nick Lovelass via Bob Haney*)

April 1943 to April 1945, and in that time the group's four squadrons primarily flew interdictory and support missions, and occasionally bombed strategic targets. The 340th hit airfields, bridges, railway lines and marshalling yards, roads, supply depots, troop concentrations, gun emplacements and factories in Greece, Yugoslavia, Albania, Austria, Bulgaria, Tunisia, Sicily, Italy and France. It also dropped propaganda leaflets behind enemy lines.

In June 1943 the group participated in the aerial assault on Pantelleria and Lampedusa, and the following month it bombed the German evacuation beaches near Messina. In September 1943 it helped establish the Salerno beachhead.

Between January and June 1944, the 340th supported the Allied drive on Rome, and in August the group was involved in the invasion of southern France. In the autumn it flew numerous missions to northern Italy to bomb targets in the Po River Valley, and the Brenner Pass was attacked from

B-25C '7F' of the 487th BS nears a light flak belt (note the black puffs of smoke) over Tunisia in early 1943. Flak was by far an aircrew's worst enemy

This 340th BG B-25C was named *VESUVIANNA – SHE DONE ME WRONG* in reference to the 22 March 1944 eruption of Mt Vesuvius that all but wiped out the group

B-25C-10 42-32278/'7K' *The Early Bird* served with the 487th BS until it was destroyed by the Mt Vesuvius eruption. This aircraft's nickname, and dubious artwork, lived on with subsequent B-25s (see page ten) (*all three photos on this page via Harry D George Jr*)

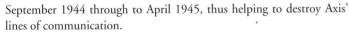

This photo gallery features 11 of the 13 B-25Js flown by the 487th BS that featured the so-called 'Dogface' nose art renditions. Flying from Corsica in mid-1944, the 487th was duly nicknamed the 'Dogface Squadron', these renditions having been done in the style of the famed World War 2 cartoonist Bill Mauldin. They paid tribute to the ground troops, which were highly respected by the unit. Mauldin drew 13 pictures, in colour, of his frontline characters. Some had snow on their helmets, some had old or young faces, a few looked sheepish – and all were bearded. These drawings served as models for the artwork painted on the noses of the aircraft, and the originals for each B-25 were placed inside the individual bombers (*all via Harry D George Jr*)

September 1944 through to April 1945, thus helping to destroy Axis' lines of communication.

During its brief existence, the 340th seemed to suffer more at the hands of Mother Nature than the Axis, being all but wiped out on two occasions through natural disasters. The first setback occurred prior to the group shipping out to North Africa when, in late 1942, the 340th was wiped out by a cyclone while still in training in South Carolina. Some 14 aeroplanes were lost in total thanks to a hailstorm that accompanied the severe weather front that moved in from the Atlantic.

340th BG B-25C *Sahara Sue* is about to receive its mission load of four 1000-lb bombs. Bomb runs usually lasted about four minutes from doors open to doors closed. When dodging fighters and flak bursts, four minutes seemed like a lifetime – and it often was (*Harry D George Jr*)

The group duly re-equipped with borrowed and/or new B-25s – a process it would carry out no less than three times during the war!

On 22 March 1944 Mt Vesuvius erupted. Although the volcano had shown signs of activity in the weeks prior to it blowing up, the group, stationed near to Pompeii, was not too concerned – after all there was a war going on. However, when Vesuvius erupted, group personnel found themselves lucky to escape with the shirts still on their backs. Hot ash and brimstone destroyed all of the aeroplanes that were parked on the field, resulting in 'Axis Sally' (the MTO's 'Tokyo Rose') gleefully announcing to the world over the air waves that the 340th was 'Fineto'. The group re-equipped with borrowed B-25s and returned to action from Paestum airfield, south of Salerno, three days later.

The 340th was one of the first units to drop phosphorous bombs against AA artillery positions prior to a bombing run. 'Axis Sally' told

B-25J-5 43-28074/'7C' of the 487th BS was one of the 13 'Dogface' aircraft flown by the unit (and is one of the pair not featured in the gallery on page 75). The veteran bomber is seen on its landing approach to its base on Corsica in late 1944. B-25 pilots had to complete 70 missions before they were deemed eligible to go home. Their counterparts in the heavy bomber groups rotated back to the US after 25 missions, however. Obviously senior USAAF commanders believed that B-25s flew less into harm's way than B-17s and B-24s (*R Besecker Collection*)

the men of the unit through her radio broadcasts that the use of this weapon was considered a breach of the Geneva Conference, and that all crewmembers participating in the phosphorous raids that were shot down would be subjected to the death penalty upon capture. She also advised that further retribution was in order, and that Germany planned to attack the 340th's base on Corsica. Shortly thereafter, the Luftwaffe bombed the airfield (as discussed elsewhere in this chapter).

It should be mentioned that many men serving with the 57th BW found out their unit assignments from 'Axis Sally' via her propaganda broadcasts prior to being officially informed by the USAAF!

In April 1944 the group converted to the Norden bombsight, which caused problems within the 340th, since the sight was suited to high altitude missions that required a longer bomb run. At medium altitude (10,000 ft or so), longer bomb runs were considered to be suicidal.

On 13 May the 340th BG's facility at Alesan, on Corsica, was severely attacked by the Luftwaffe. The raid caused many casualties, and extensive damage was inflicted on the group's aeroplanes and other equipment. The operation gave every indication of having been thoroughly planned and executed.

The gun control room of the anti-aircraft batteries defending the airfield reported spotting the first enemy aircraft at 0335 hrs, which ground observers identified as an RAF Beaufighter – possibly a captured example employed by the enemy as a pathfinder. A few minutes later the aeroplane dropped flares on the airfield, followed almost immediately by further aircraft releasing more flares. These thoroughly illuminated the airfield, and allowed the German bombers to accurately drop numerous demolition and anti-personnel bombs, including delayed action devices.

Below and bottom
An unidentified Mitchell (top photo) and B-25J-1 43-27703/'8W' of the 488th BS were just two of the many 340th BG aircraft that were destroyed during the successful Luftwaffe raid on the Corsican airfield of Alesan on the night of 13 May 1944 (*Boeing*)

As the attack progressed, the enemy resorted to strafing runs, dropping to within a few feet of the ground. Attacking aeroplanes were identified as Ju 88s and Fw 190s, as well as possibly Bf 109s, Do 217s and He 111s. Some of the fighters strafed AA positions on the beach bordering the airfield and on the ridges to the north and west.

The attacking force was estimated at 20 to 30 aeroplanes, which specifically targeted the airfield proper, its fuel dump, the ground radio station trailer due west of the centre of the field, the adjacent highway, the operations intelligence building close by and the 489th BS area about three-quarters of a mile north of the field. Finally, 'frag' bombs intended for the HQ tent area two miles north of the field missed their target and fell into the sea a few hundred yards off shore.

The attack lasted about one hour and fifteen minutes, which was the total elapsed time from when the first enemy aircraft was plotted to when the last one departed.

Prior to attacking the airfield, the aeroplanes seemed to initally fly over the target at about 3000 ft. However, once the field had been lit up by flares dropped by the pathfinders, and by burning aircraft, and when the AA barrage was found to be ineffective, the attackers dove down to as low as 50 ft on their strafing runs. Two courses were flown during the attack, although some aircraft seemed to come in from different directions after circling off the target. These courses were approximately north-west to south-east and south-east to north-west.

Most of the 340th's engineering, armament and ordnance personnel had their tents on the airfield proper, and although they had the use of slit trenches, casualties were exceedingly high from the bombing and strafing – not to mention their own B-25s blowing up, many with full bomb loads.

The attack had been preceded by a raid on Poretta airfield (some 15 miles north of Alesan Field) at 0100 hrs, leaving 25 Spitfires destroyed and a number of men killed.

The attack on Alesan Field was a devastating blow to the 340th BG.

Yet despite being dealt another serious setback, the 'hard luck' 340th BG remained in-theatre until VE-Day, finally returning to the US in July-August 1945. It was inactivated on 7 November 1945.

COMBAT ACCOUNTS

On 22 June 1944, Lt Harry D George co-piloted 487th BS B-25J-5 43-27656 *McKINLEY JR. HIGH* on a mission against a railway bridge at Gricigliana, on the main line running south from Bologna to Florence. The following account of that sortie has been taken from the biographical volume *Georgio Italiano: An American Pilot's Unlikely Tuscan Adventure* (Trafford Publishing

Another 340th BG B-25J severely damaged in the Alesan raid, this aircraft was later repaired and put back into service. The attack on the Corsican base was one of the worst raids suffered by any B-25 group during the entire MTO campaign (*USAF*)

With his left hand resting on his bomber's fuselage, 487th BS pilot Harry D George poses with the crew of B-25J-5 43-27656/'7C' *McKINLEY JR. HIGH* prior to its fateful mission on 22 June 1944 (*Harry D George Jr*)

An overall view of the newly-delivered B-25J-5 43-27656/'7C' *McKINLEY JR. HIGH.* This bomber was bought for the USAAF by students from McKinley Jr High School in Muncie, Indiana, who raised $250,000 from the sales of War Bonds. Its premature demise in combat was unfortunate to say the least (*Harry D George Jr*)

2000), written by Harry D George Jr, who reconstructed the events of the mission following an interview with his father. In part, his father's recollection of this mission is as follows;

'That bridge was a tough target – a short, single-track structure nestling in a very narrow valley between two steep mountains. It was a crucial target. That rail line was the main supply route for the German troops in the south. For much of its length, tunnels protected the track. Flat stretches of track are more easily hit, but they are also more easily, and quickly, repaired. Taking out the bridge at Gricigliana (Gri-chil-yana) would disrupt German re-supply efforts for some time. That, in turn, was crucial to winning the battle on the ground at the front just north of Rome. That was our job – blowing up road bridges, railroad bridges and marshalling yards to keep the German re-supply efforts paralysed.

'That afternoon found us gathered around our aeroplane, B-25 "7C", named after McKinley Jr High in Muncie, Indiana. It was so named in honour of the junior high school that had raised the $250,000 needed to finance it by selling War Bonds. The aircraft was a brand new J-model, which had just been issued to the 340th BG for combat not even a month earlier. It was still unpainted.

'We had just come from the briefing, and the briefing officer had not painted a very rosy picture of what was in store for us. Twelve batteries of German 88 mm AA artillery guns protected the target. Our group had tried to destroy this bridge on three previous occasions, the last of which had been just a few hours before. All three attempts met with disastrous results – a lot of aeroplanes damaged by flak, yet the bridge remained intact.

'As a result of our misses, the Germans also knew our attack pattern and altitude – from the west at 10,000 ft.

'We crawled up into the aeroplane and started the engines. Tom Casey was the pilot and Ed Dombrowski the bombardier. We taxied onto the runway and took our position in the line. We took off from Alesan, on Corsica, at around 1830 hrs. After the formation had been assembled, we headed north-east.

'We were in the second of two boxes of six aeroplanes from our squadron. The 310th BG had three boxes of six B-25s right ahead of us, making the formation 30-strong overall. We approached the target at about 1915 hrs.

'The flak was very heavy and accurate, exploding at precisely 10,000 ft. From the IP, the aeroplanes had to be flown straight and level until the bombs were released. This was crucial if the bombardier was to stand any chance of first sighting and then hitting the target. No evasive action was allowed. Those two or three minutes were the terror-filled times on every mission, and this particular sortie was one of the worst. We were goddamned sitting ducks – especially those of us at the back of the formation.

'The aeroplanes ahead of us were engulfed in black flak-burst smoke. I could see the bombs leave the lead ship. Ours quickly followed. The instant after we dropped our bombs, we were hit by flak. Our aeroplane shook as though it were trying to tear itself apart. The left engine had been shot away. We were hit amidships, too. Fire was sweeping back throughout the aeroplane. The fuel lines had been hit, and it wouldn't be long until the tanks would blow. The hydraulic lines were also hit and the boosted flight controls were lost. I was now forced to literally manhandle it.

'The right engine was sputtering and coughing. It started running away, which was a pilot's worst nightmare, because at some point the prop speed would become too great for the blades and they would disintegrate and fly off – probably into the aeroplane and they were right next to the cockpit, not more than a foot away!

'The pilot, Casey, who was sitting just to my left, was hit in several places by the flak. Part of his head was missing, and his blood was everywhere – splattered all over the inside of the windshield.

'I took the controls and issued the order to jump over the interphone. It was all I could do to keep the aeroplane level. The best I could hope for was to keep the aeroplane level long enough for the crew to get out. That's what I did.

'I was using every ounce of strength I had to keep the aeroplane under control, get it safely out of the formation, and to keep it level while we were descending. We were losing speed and altitude fast. I looked over at Casey and figured him for dead. No one could be alive with that much of their head gone. Just then, he turned his eyes

McKINLEY JR. HIGH goes down streaming smoke from its wing tanks. Note how much of the left vertical tail surface is missing, and that the left gear leg has extended. This photograph was taken from another B-25 on the same 22 June 1944 mission that had seen the 487th BS sent to bomb the railway bridge at Gricigliana (*Harry D George Jr*)

toward me and said, in one last act of heroism, "For God's sake George, get out!" and then promptly died. I climbed out of the seat, stood there for a second or two at the most, and went down through the fire and out the hatch.

'Ha! I had refused parachute training. I was a young smart-ass and thought that parachuting was too damned dangerous to practice. If my life depended on it I'd jump, but not just for the hell of it. How much could there be to pulling a ripcord?

'Well, I jumped once, and only once, in my career – on 22 June 1944.

'To make sure I had cleared the aeroplane, I waited at least ten seconds before I pulled the cord. Nothing happened! "Ah shit!" I thought. I had survived getting hit bad in the aeroplane and was now going to die because my goddamned 'chute didn't open.

'Everything happened so fast. The aeroplane was probably at 8000 ft when I jumped. Between waiting to pull the ripcord and the problem with the pilot 'chute not opening right away, leaving me to free-fall some 6000 ft, I guessed I was at 2000 ft when the 'chute finally did open. There isn't a lot of sky, or time, left at 2000 ft.

'I looked at the aeroplane. Not only had the left engine been blown away, the left landing gear had come down. Most of the left tail and rudder were gone as well. I'd heard about a B-25 getting back to base on one engine and one tail with no hydraulics, but it had taken both the pilot and co-pilot struggling with all their might to do it. I felt good that alone I had been able to keep the ship out of a spin and flying level for long enough to allow everyone who was alive to get out.

'The aeroplane's right engine or wing tank exploded shortly after I jumped and the B-25 was screaming toward the ground to the south of me. I couldn't watch the crash, and I looked away.

'I hit some tree branches upon landing. I stood up. My right foot was jammed, but I could walk. That was enough for the moment.'

As it happened, Lt Harry D George had landed far behind enemy lines. He was subsequently reported as a Missing in Action member of the 340th BG. He spent nearly three months in Axis territory, surviving his ordeal with the help of Italian locals, and by living in caves until September, when he was returned to US control.

Fellow B-25 pilot 1Lt William P Laney, of the 486th BS, flew 51 combat missions and received a Distinguished Flying Cross and six Air Medals. He racked up 123 hours and 35 minutes during his 51 combat missions, flown between 17 February and 15 August 1944. Laney attacked Axis targets in France and Italy on all of his sorties .

William Laney passed away on 18 September 1993, and his

There were several Mitchells called *BOTTOMS-UP* in the 486th BS, this particular example being B-25J-5 43-27800/'6V'. Unfortunately, none of these crewmen had been identified as this volume went to press. Another *BOTTOMS-UP* (B-25J-143-4082/ '6V') crashed into the mountains of northern Corsica moments after taking off at night on 18 March 1945. Although the wreckage was discovered several weeks later, no trace of the crew was ever found. Note the patches of natural metal skinning where the blister guns have been removed from this machine (*Fred Hayner Collection*)

Nicknamed *YAHOUDI*, B-25J-1 43-27478 was yet another multi-mission veteran of the 340th BG. While an aircraft's name usually came from its commander, both learned artists and novice 'wannabes' generated its nose art (*Harry D George Jr*)

Mitchell units in the MTO did not always get fighter escorts during their bombing missions, as the tight box formations that they flew in were deemed to be all but impregnable to Axis fighters. And by mid 1944, enemy aircraft were rarely encountered over northern Italy in any case. However, on this occasion a flight of B-25s from the 487th FS (including B-25J-1 43-27478/'7J' *YAHOUDI*) have been joined by a trio of drop tank-equipped P-47Ds from the 350th FG's 346th FS (*USAF via Harry D George Jr*)

grandson, Mike Laney, relates some of his grandfather's exploits in the following account;

'Lt William P "Lightning" Laney was assigned to the 486th BS on 17 January 1944, and he flew his first 11 missions with seasoned pilots (including Lt Donald K "Deke" Slayton, one of the original seven *Mercury* Astronauts) before eventually flying the lead position on many of the missions. On his 34th mission, on 19 May, while bombing a railway bridge at Arezzo, in Italy, his aeroplane ("6K") took a hit which caused an electrical fire that made it impossible for his crew to salvo their bombs. During this same mission, the 486th BS had three B-25s shot down.

'The army had decided to have an exchange programme in which infantry officers were brought to the 340th BG to gain a greater appreciation of what the medium bombers were doing for them on the ground. One major (an artillery observer) who flew with Lt J J McCormick decided that being on the ground was best, and that these pilots were crazy to be doing what they did. Lt McCormick was asked to go with the major to the front to gain a greater appreciation for being on the ground. However, McCormick had by then completed his 70 missions and received his orders to go home. Lt Laney was the lucky guy who got to go to the front in McCormick's place. I'm sure

B-25J-1 43-27633/'7Q' of the 487th BS unloads its four 1000-lb bombs over the Brenner Pass. Axis forces used the pass to transport replacement war equipment and personnel to the front. Some MTO-based B-25s ventured so far afield into eastern Europe (southern Czechoslovakia and northern Yugoslavia, for example) in 1944-45 that they were effectively bombing targets technically assigned to units operating in the ETO!
(*Harry D George Jr*)

he had similar opinions of being on the ground as the major had about flying through flak!

'After 13 April Laney was assigned Aeroplane Command for B-25J-1 43-4061/'6K', nicknamed *I'LL TAKE YOU HOME AGAIN KATHLEEN II*, with T/Sgt Rocco 'Rocky' Petrozzi as its crew chief. This aeroplane went on to complete more than 100 missions.

'My grandfather was known to all of his squadronmates as "Lightning" Laney. He earned this nickname for two reasons. Firstly, he was from Monroe, North Carolina, and therefore came from a slower pace of life, and secondly, he had a reputation for his ability to "get the hell out of Dodge" as soon as his B-25 had salvoed its bombs. This made Laney a popular lead pilot .

'During his 51st combat mission (bombing bridges at Avignon, in France) on 15 August 1944, Laney witnessed his best friend's

With smiles for the camera, three 340th BG gunners – Frank Pehrson (left), Bob Hertel (centre) and unknown, head for their B-25 on Corsica in 1944. Note the flak jackets and steel helmets worn/carried by two of the gunners, and the belted 0.50-cal 'slugs' slung over the shoulders of all three men
(*Frank Pehrson via Bob Haney*)

488th BS B-25J-15 43-27504/'8K', flown by 1Lt Marvin Stoff, was one of 24 Mitchells from the 340th BG that bombed Padua, in Italy, on 10 December 1944. Each aircraft dropped four 1000-lb bombs on marshalling yards, tracks and bridges. The bombing altitude was 10,200 ft, and although the flak was heavy, all the B-25s returned safely to Alesan airfield, on Corsica (*via Author*)

aeroplane ('6T', flown by John P "Jack" Hoschar) take a direct hit, and all six men on board were killed.

'As his grandson, I derive great pride from 1Lt William P Laney's service to his country. Although he would say that he was only doing his job, and he wasn't a hero, he will always be a hero to me.'

S/Sgt Dana H Craig also served with the 486th BS, seeing combat as as a Top Turret Gunner. Here, he remembers the Anzio missions;

'Not too many people have talked much about the raids on Anzio. Maybe that's because they were so costly to our B-25 crews over there.

'The Anzio flights literally scared the hell out of me. Yet sometimes when we left Corsica on a mission to Anzio in the bright blue sky, it often seemed like it was going to be a beautiful day. That's until we looked ahead and saw the big black clouds over our target area – flak bursts around preceding aircraft. My immediate thought was "why do we have to fly into that?" Anzio was such a concentrated target that it seemed like everyone was in on the act, and for the part, it was true.

'The worst part was the pre-flight instructions during briefings that told us that our targets were only a few hundred yards from friendly positions. That told me that we'd have to fly straight and level for a longer than normal amount of time. My heart goes out to all the aircrews that shared the Anzio experiences.'

2Lt Victor Ramirez was stationed on Corsica with the 488th BS from December 1944 through to March 1945. His most memorable mission was as follows:

This 340th BG B-25J, viewed from directly above by a second Mitchell, will soon make its own bomb run at the smoke-shrouded target some 9000 ft below. Note the crater-marked fields just short of the target, which was one of the many road/rail bridges hit by the 340th in northern Italy (*USAF*)

'In early 1944 in a briefing in Columbia, South Carolina, we were told about the new and improved B-25J with "all electric systems". This new aircraft had two separate bomb releases for redundancy, one on either side of the B-25 (but with no manual bomb release for back up). Someone asked "what if both systems fail?" The North American Aviation technical rep answered, "there's only a one in a thousand chance of that happening. That's why we put them on different sides of the aeroplane", he added. Well, that did happen to yours truly, on our aeroplane. We were the "one in a thousand".

'On my 39th mission, on 30 March 1945, our target was the Ora railway bridge in north Italy. We got hit by AA artillery fire over the target and lost one of our engines with a full bomb load still aboard, which, of course, we weren't able to jettison because both of the electric bomb release switches were destroyed. We were unable to maintain altitude on one engine, a full crew of six and all our bombs, so we desperately tried to limp back to friendly skies.

'We were able to fly as far as Venice from the Brenner Pass area, where the entire crew, and yours truly, bailed out. We were all captured and taken prisoner the very same day. So much for the B-25J's new all-electric system.

'Believe it or not, we actually hitch-hiked back up the Brenner Pass with our captors to a German prison camp in Moosburg, Austria. So, for the rest of the war our home was *Stalag Luft* 7A. We were all finally liberated by Gen Patton's troops.'

57th BW

The large entity that became known as the 57th Bomb Wing (BW) was first activated on 6 November 1940 as the 8th Pursuit Wing at Maxwell Field, Alabama. It was not designated as the 57th BW until 6 April 1942 by authority of the US War Department. Now a part of the Ninth Air Force, the 57th duly moved from the Egyptian airfield at El Kabrit to Deversoir, in eastern Egypt, on 5 June 1942.

Two months later, on 23 August, Ninth Air Force headquarters ordered the 57th to move to Tunis, Tunisia, where it was reassigned to the Twelfth Air Force. That same month the wing took charge of its first Mitchell-equipped bomb group, the 12th BG. The group was duly followed into the MTO by the 340th, 310th, 321st and 319th BGs.

At one time or another, all five of the aforementioned medium bomb groups were controlled by the 57th BW. The 12th was joined by the 340th BG on 1 November 1943, and three days later the 321st was assigned to the wing. On 1 January 1944, however, these three groups were reassigned to XII Bomber Command. Two months later, on 1 March, the latter organisation became a 'paper-unit', and its resources – including the 321st and 340th BGs – were transferred back to the 57th BW, which for the first time became operational as an independent wing assigned to the Twelfth Air Force.

The 310th BG joined the 57th on 15 March 1944, by which time the 12th BG had moved to eastern India, having been reassigned to the Tenth Air Force for action in the CBI. On 10 November 1944 the 319th BG – then converting from B-26s to B-25s – joined the 57th. With the relatively late arrival of the 319th, and the earlier departure

Typical of the Mitchells controlled by the 57th BW, B-25J-1 43-27729/ '8S' of the 488th BS/340th BG is seen on its final approach to Alesan airfield, on Corsica, following yet another mission against targets in the Po River Valley in March 1944 (*Norm Taylor Collection*)

Veteran B-25C-5 42-53389/'7J' of the 487th BS heads for the Brenner Pass in early 1944, along with other Mitchells from the 340th BG. Nicknamed *OLD BUGS*, this machine was almost certainly destroyed by the Vesuvius eruption on 22 March 1944 (*Harry D George Jr*)

of the 12th, the 57th BW now controlled four B-25 groups, each with four squadrons.

But this force level was maintained only temporarily, for in late December the 319th started to phase out of the MTO after receiving orders to return to the US for retraining on the A-26 Invader, prior to being sent into action in the Pacific.

During the period 8-10 January 1945, the 319th departed its base on Corsica and began its return flight to the US. The group's assignment to the 57th BW was terminated on 10 January.

Following the cessation of hostilities in Europe in May 1945, the three remaining B-25-equipped bomb groups in the MTO prepared to return home. The first to go, between 16-26 July, was the 340th BG, and it was followed by the 310th and 321st BGs between 1-15 August.

With its wartime work now finished, the 57th BW was inactivated on 12 September 1945. It had seen both VE- and VJ-Days come and go, and had played a relatively brief, but nonetheless important role in securing an Allied victory in Europe. Although it had only seen some 15 months of combat, the wing had earned eight campaign streamers based on either actual combat or presence in the combat zone. These included Naples-Foggia (no combat but in zone), Anzio (combat operations), Rome-Arno (combat operations in zone), southern France (combat operations), North Apennines (combat operations), EAME theatre (combat operations, Yugoslavia), Central Europe (combat operations) and the Po River Valley (combat operations).

Three of its groups had earned Distinguished Unit Citations, namely the 310th BG for action over Ora, in Italy, on 10 March 1945, the 321st BG for action over France on 18 August 1944, and the 340th BG for action over Italy on 23 September 1944.

COMING HOME

Amongst the veteran aircrewmen of the 57th BW that headed home following VE-Day was T/Sgt John Jarvis, a radioman with the 445th BS/321st BG. He remembers;

'From our last base of operations on Corsica we flew our battered, war-weary bird back to the states soon after VE-Day, stopping in Africa and South America, among other places, for fuel. We were ill-prepared for the long flight home because we had no navigator, so we were forced to pick one up before heading out. A navigator was absolutely essential because we had to find Ascension Island for our first refuelling. That particular island in the Atlantic Ocean was so small – only 34 square miles – that it wasn't even shown on the world map we had. We had to get a map that showed it!

'Our pilot, Maj Vaughn, knew the first heading to fly after take-off. After about an hour, he asked the navigator for a new heading. He did not get it. The navigator said he was working on it. To cut a long story short, the major repeatedly asked for headings and got none. Things got pretty hectic. The "navigator", a second lieutenant, confessed that he was not a navigator after all – he had just said he was to get a flight home!

'Maj Vaughn called me on the intercom and asked me to make a stab at navigating us. I called Bolling Field, using Morse code, and got the wind speed aloft for our flight. I then applied dead reckoning. All of us were understandably apprehensive. I gave our pilot corrective headings along the way, using the figures from Bolling, and kept my fingers crossed.

'We finally saw Ascension Island on the far horizon and headed straight for it. Maj Vaughn landed the aeroplane on the island's humpback runway. After we came to stop at the end of the runway, he really ate out that lieutenant. He did a pretty fair job of it too!

'The crew members congratulated me for my navigating expertise. Expertise? It was pure dumb luck. From the island, we flew on without a navigator. This was safe to do because it was impossible not to make landfall at some place or another on a continent as large as South America. After we left South America, as soon as we were near enough to home to receive stateside commercial radio broadcast stations, the aeroplane's Radio Direction Finder was used for the rest of the flight.'

Unit and type unknown, *Screaming Meemie!*, and its unnamed crew, pose for the mandatory scrapbook shot during their tour of the MTO. B-25s had six-man crews, and these fellows are wearing typical attire for the theatre. A standard crew consisted, for the most part, of a pilot (always the aeroplane commander), co-pilot, bombardier, navigator, top turret gunner/radioman and tail gunner. The waist guns were usually manned by navigators, top turret gunners and bombardiers, depending on whichever two men were most available (*Bob Haney Collection*)

B-25 MTO BOMB GROUP/BOMB SQUADRON MARKINGS

12th BG

81st BS – white numerals 1-25 (black after 3/44)

82nd BS – white numerals 26-50 (black after 3/44)

83rd BS – white numerals 51-75 (black after 3/44)

434th BS – white numerals 76-100 (black after 3/44)

310th BG*

379th BS – wide yellow band over narrower white band

380th BS – wide yellow band over narrower blue band

381st BS – wide yellow band over narrower red band

428th BS – wide yellow band over narrower yellow band

* before 1944 the 310th BG had a single yellow stripe on the tails

319th BG*

437th BS – white numerals 1-24 inside a square on cobalt blue tails

438th BS – white numerals 25-49 inside a square on cobalt blue tails

439th BS – white numerals 50-74 inside a square on cobalt blue tails

440th BS – white numerals 75-100 inside a square on cobalt blue tails

* each squadron painted their colours on the cowl rings of their aircraft – some aircraft also had wide white bands around the aft fuselage

321st BG*

445th BS – I (black numerals 01-25 after 1/45)

446th BS – 2 (black numerals 26-50 after 1/45)

447th BS – 2I (black numerals 51-75 after 1/45)

448th BS – IV (black numerals 76-100 after 1/45)

* from 1943-44 the 321st BG had red rudder tips with large roman numerals on the tails

340th BG

486th BS – white letters 6A through 6Z and white cowl rings/ prop spinners
487th BS – white letters 7A through 7Z and blue cowl rings/ prop spinners
488th BS – white letters 8A through 8Z and red cowl rings/ prop spinners
489th BS – white letters 9A through 9Z and yellow cowl rings/ prop spinners

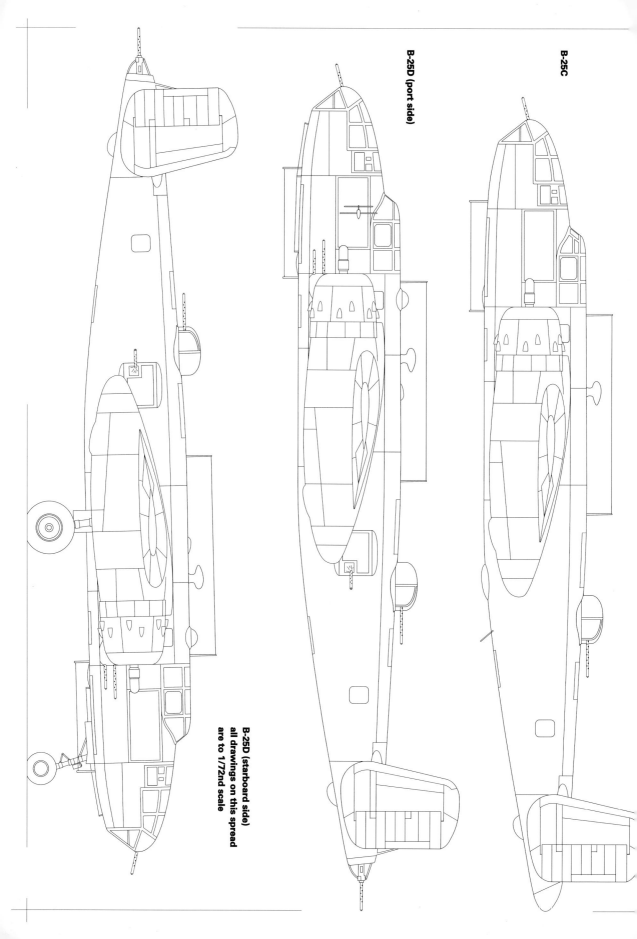

B-25C

B-25D (port side)

B-25D (starboard side)
all drawings on this spread
are to 1/72nd scale

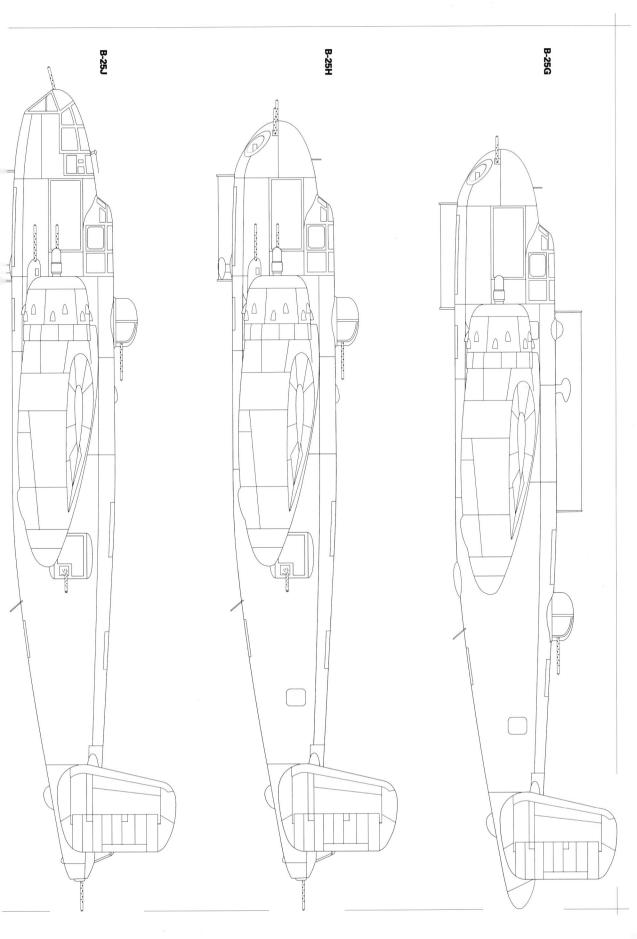

B-25J

B-25H

B-25G

COLOUR PLATES

1
B-25C 41-12480/*DESERT WARRIOR* of Capt Ralph Lower, 81st BS/12th BG, Bolling Field, Washington DC, July 1943

Named *DESERT WARRIOR* (*MOKATELAT EL-SAHARA* in Arabic script, which is also featured in the mission tally 'box'), 41-12480 completed 73 combat missions, totalling 191 hours, from Hergla, Tunisia, before it was selected to represent the medium bomb groups equipped with B-25s in the MTO during one of the many US War Bond drives undertaken by the armed forces across America. The veteran bomber was given a Hollywood-style paint job on its nose, including an extremely detailed mission log and campaign map, and sent on its way. Seven hand-picked (and mission expired) crewmembers, representing all four units in the 12th BG, manned 41-12480 during its stateside tour.

2
B-25H-1 43-4183 of 1Lt Harry Hudson, 81st BS/12th BG, Gaudo, Italy, 30 December 1943

Yet to feature bomb icons, crew names and nose art, B-25H-1 43-4183 is represented here as it appeared straight after completing its first mission – an attack on a 500-ft long Axis vessel in the Adriatic, followed by strafing runs on the wharves at Zara, in Yugoslavia. This machine was one of nine B-25s despatched by the 81st BS on this mission, these aircraft being joined by nine Mitchells from the 83rd and six from the 434th. All aircraft returned safely.

3
B-25H-1 43-4208/*VIKIN'S VICIOUS VIRGIN* of Capt Henry Vikin, 82nd BS/12th BG, Gaudo, Italy, 30 December 1943

VIKIN'S VICIOUS VIRGIN participated in a leaflet dropping mission over Atina, Italy, on 30 December 1943, this B-25 being joined by numerous others from the 82nd BS. These propaganda missions were usually flown at an altitude of about 9000 ft.

4
B-25H-1 43-4381/*DOG DAIZE* of 1Lt Jared Miller, 82nd BS/12th BG, Gaudo, Italy, 28 December 1943

On 28 December 1943, 36 B-25s from the 81st, 82nd and 434th BSs (12 aircraft each) bombed the axis landing ground at Ciampino, in Italy. The weather was good and all 36 returned safely, including *DOG DAIZE*. The colours and markings of this particular B-25H have been applied to the restored Mitchell owned by the New England Air Museum in Connecticut.

5
B-25C 41-12863 of Capt Doug Spawn, 82nd BS/12th BG, Tmed El Clel, Libya, 9 January 1943

Capt Spawn flew this B-25C on numerous occasions during his tour. On 9 January 1943, Spawn and his crew took part in a mixed formation mission with other 12th BG B-25s and Baltimore IIIs from the RAF's No 232 Wing, the aircraft bombing the Axis-held Mareth Line, in Tunisia. To the best of the author's knowledge, the late Lt Col Spawn never named his aeroplanes, or had them adorned with nose art.

6
B-25H-10 43-4909/*EATIN' KITTY* of 1Lt Charles Matheson, 82nd BS/12th BG, Foggia, Italy, 22 October 1943

EATIN' KITTY was one of 24 B-25s (six from each squadron in the 12th BG) that attacked the town of Teano, in Italy, on 22 October 1943. The aircraft pattern-bombed from 8500 to 9500 ft, and crews observed numerous direct hits on the target. Although several Mitchells were 'holed' by flak, they all returned safely to Foggia.

7
B-25J-1 43-27498/*SUNDAY PUNCH* of Capt Richard Robinson, 82nd BS/12th BG, Foggia, Italy, 24 October 1943

SUNDAY PUNCH was one of only a handful of 'solid-nosed' B-25Js to see service with the 12th BG. It was one of 24 Mitchells (six from each squadron) that the 12th BG sortied on 24 October 1943 to bomb the town of Formia, in Italy. Three aircraft, including *SUNDAY PUNCH*, were flak holed on this mission, but all returned safely to base.

8
B-25H-1 43-4357/*Leroy's Joy* of 1Lt Leroy Roberts, 82nd BS/12th BG, Foggia, Italy, 19 November 1943

Leroy's Joy was part of a 24-aircraft formation (one six-aeroplane box from each squadron) that attacked the German barracks complex west of Travnik, in Yugoslavia on 19 November 1943. One B-25 also dropped leaflets, and all returned safely.

9
B-25D-10 41-30344/*PINK PETUNIA* of 1Lt John Stolk, 83rd BS/12th BG, Medenine, Tunisia, 2 April 1943

One of 18 aircraft that dropped British 250-lb bombs on enemy positions in the Wadi Afarit region of Libya on 2 April 1943, *PINK PETUNIA* endured heavy AA artillery which holed 14 B-25s. There were no casualties, however, and all aircraft returned safely to Medenine.

10
B-25C-1 41-13120 of Capt George Simmons, 434th BS/12th BG, Sfax, Tunisia, 6 May 1943

This B-25C was one of 18 aircraft despatched from Sfax on a navigation-training mission to Castel Benito and back on 6 May 1943 – nine of these machines were from the 83rd BS. Two days later,

41-13120 was involved in a combat mission against dispersed enemy aircraft on Pantelleria island.

11
B-25J-1 43-27676/*THE LITTLE KING* of 1Lt Howard King, 380th BS/310th BG, Philippeville, Algeria, 10 November 1944

THE LITTLE KING flew no less than 121 combat missions before ending its career at Fano, in Italy, following the end of the MTO campaign in May 1945. Its original pilot was 1Lt Howard C King, hence its name. The Mitchell on display at the Museum of Aviation, in Georgia, is presently painted as 43-27676.

12
B-25J-15 44-28925/*HOW 'BOOT THAT!?* of Capt Joseph Luchford, 380th BS/310th BG, Ghisonaccia, Corsica, 23 November 1944

HOW 'BOOT THAT!? was accepted by the USAAF in August 1944, and from the autumn of that year through to the late spring of 1945, this aeroplane completed more than 80 combat missions over northern Italy, southern Austria and Yugoslavia. Miraculously, it survived the mass post-war scrapping of combat aircraft, and 44-28925 can today be seen on display at the Cavanaugh Flight Museum in Addison, Texas. It is one of only a handful of genuine combat-seasoned USAAF B-25s still in existence.

13
B-25C-15 42-32505 of 2Lt William Wolfe, 381st BS/310th BG, Temime, Tunisia, 27 August 1943

Depicted here prior to its assignment of a regular crew, this B-25C completed its first combat mission on 27 August 1943. It was one of 36 Mitchells that dropped six 500-lb bombs apiece on the Benevento marshalling yards from a height of 10,050 ft. They were escorted throughout the mission by 26 P-38 Lightnings from the 82nd FG. The return flight was uneventful, although two aircraft had to make refuelling stops on Sicily.

14
B-25J-10 43-36099 of 1Lt John Marlow, 440th BS/319th BG, Djedeida, Tunisia, 7 July 1944

On 7 July 1944 this B-25J was part of a 36-aeroplane formation (18 apiece from the 439th and the 440th BSs) sent to bomb rail targets in the Brenner Pass. All the aircraft carried, and dropped, four 1000-lb general-purpose bombs.

15
B-25J-1 43-27698 of Capt Henry Miller, 445th BS/321st BG, Falconara, Italy, 10 January 1945

PEGGY LOU and 17 other B-25s in three six-aeroplane boxes dropped 20-lb fragmentation bombs on the marshalling yards at Padua, Italy on 10 January 1945. Flak was judged to be light to medium in intensity, and all aeroplanes returned safely to Falconara.

16
B-25C-1 41-13207/*OH-7* of 2Lt Charles Irwin, 445th BS/321st BG, Oujda, French Morocco, 14 February 1943

On 14 February 1943 *OH-7* was forced to make a wheels-up belly landing after a complete loss of hydraulic fluid. One of six 445th BS Mitchells that had strafed and bombed Axis shipping intercepted in the southern Mediterranean just north of Libya, *OH-7* had been badly damaged by flak during the attack.

17
B-25J-1 43-27747/*PEGGY LOU* of 1Lt Michael Murphy, 445th BS/321st BG, Soliman, Tunisia, 27 August 1943

On 27 August 1943, this B-25J ran into heavy flak whilst dropping six 500-lb bombs on the Benevento railroad yards near Naples, in southern Italy. It was holed more than 80 times, but still returned safely across the Mediterranean to Soliman. Three other B-25s in this 18-aeroplane formation were not so lucky, being shot down over the target.

18
B-25J-1 43-27475 of 1Lt Donald Nickelson, 447th BS/321st BG, Falconara, Italy, 11 November 1944

This B-25J, along with 17 others in three six-aeroplane boxes, dropped 'frag' bombs on troop convoys in the Brenner Pass on 11 November 1944. No losses were suffered, but one B-25J from the the 447th had about 60 per cent of its right vertical fin and rudder blown off. Despite having to fight to control their ill-handling B-25, the crew still managed to limp home with only a single working rudder.

19
B-25D-15 41-30538/*SHAD RACK* of 2Lt Douglas Daly, 447th BS/321st BG, Oujda, French Morocco, 22 December 1942

SHAD RACK attacked vessels in and around Tunis and Bizerta harbours on 22 December 1942, the vessels being both strafed and bombed during the mission. Some 24 447th BS B-25s and an identical number of Mitchells from the 446th BS took part in this mission, during which as many as 60 vessels were seen. Numerous ships were seen to be listing and/or smoking as these aircraft headed back to Oujda.

20
B-25J-15 44-29090/*WHO CARES?* of 1Lt Billy McVee, 486th BS/340th BG, Rimini, Italy, 13 May 1944

WHO CARES? was one of the many 340th BG B-25s that was shot up and/or completely destroyed during the successful Luftwaffe air raid on Alesan airfield, on the island of Corsica, on the night of 13 May 1944. With its entire right side ripped open, and its right vertical tail/rudder blown off, 44-29090 was declared fit only for salvage and scrapped on site.

21

B-25J-1 43-27475/ *THE ALICE L* **of 2Lt Johnny Dickenson, 486th BS/340th BG, Rimini, Italy, 25 August 1944**

Although holed quite severely (more than 30 times), *ALICE L* returned safely from the 25 August 1944 attack on the Brenner Pass railway line near the town of Rovereto, in Italy. The bomber had been part of a 24-aeroplane formation comprised of four six-ship boxes. Two B-25s failed to return from this mission, having fallen victim to intense flak.

22

B-25J-5 43-27900/ *BOTTOMS-UP II* **of 1Lt Clarence Morton, 486th BS/340th BG, Gaudo, Italy, 12 March 1944**

On 12 March 1944, *BOTTOMS-UP II* participated in its 39th mission. After dropping its four 1000-lb bombs on the Ora railway bridge in northern Italy, 43-27900 was hit in the right engine by flak, forcing the pilot to shut it down. The bomber was subsequently able to make an emergency landing at an Allied fighter base on the northern tip of Corsica.

23

B-25C 41-12472 of 1Lt George Wamsley, 487th BS/340th BG, Landing Ground 99 (El Kabrit), Egypt, 12 December 1942

This B-25C was lost, along with its entire crew, on 12 December 1942 while on an anti-shipping strafing mission. Flying in the trailing six-aeroplane box, with two other six-bomber boxes ahead of it, the B-25 was attacked by a Bf 109. The 487th BS was operating out of El Kabrit, in Egypt, at the time.

24

B-25J-1 43-4065/ *G.I. JOES* **of Capt Joseph P Turner, 487th BS/340th BG, Rimini, Italy, 24 July 1944**

This B-25J was one of thirteen specially-adorned 487th BS/340th BG Mitchells that featured the so-called 'Dogface' nose art renditions. These artworks, done in the style of the famed World War 2 cartoonist Bill Mauldin, paid tribute to the ground troops, which were highly respected by the 340th BG. Mauldin drew 13 pictures, in colour, of his frontline characters (this aircraft was the first so adorned). Some had snow on their helmets, others had old or young faces, a few looked sheepish – and all were bearded. These drawings served as models for the ones painted on the noses of the aircraft themselves. The originals for each B-25 were placed inside the aircraft.

25

B-25J-1 43-27704 of Capt Jack Ram, 487th BS/340th BG, Rimini, Italy, 17 August 1944

This B-25J participated in the attack on the Vichy French battleship *Strasbourg* on on 17 August 1944. The heavy barrage of flak thrown up by the ship, and port defences at Toulon, damaged 27 aircraft, including '7A', but all returned safely. The

very next day the 321st BG successfully sunk the *Strasbourg*, a *La Galissonniere* class cruiser and a submarine.

26

B-25D (serial unknown) of Flg Off M C Burger RAF, 487th BS/340th BG, Landing Ground 99 (El Kabrit), Egypt, 2 November 1942

This B-25D, based at LG 99 at the time and flown by an RAF exchange pilot, participated in the pivotal Battle of El Alamein.

27

B-25J-1 43-27504 of 1Lt Marvin Stoff, 488th BS/340th BG, Alesan, Corsica, 10 December 1944

This B-25J, and 23 others from the 488th BS, bombed Padua, Italy, on 10 December 1944. They each dropped four 1000-lb bombs on marshalling yards, tracks and bridges. The day's bombing altitude was 10,200 ft, and although the flak was reportedly heavy, all the B-25s returned safely to Alesan.

28

B-25J-1 43-27638/ *BRIEFING TIME* **of Capt Bus Taylor, 489th BS/340th BG, Rimini, Italy, 15 November 1944**

BRIEFING TIME flew 126 missions, and T/Sgt Joe Moore was its crew chief towards the end of its career. He first 'wrenched' on a B-25 named *LITTLE JOE*, which was lost in combat, then on a few others, before joining *BRIEFING TIME*. After 43-27638 completed its 126th mission without having experienced a single premature return through mechanical fault, Joe offered to paint the name *QUITTING TIME!* on her nose. B-25J-25 44-29939, has been restored by the Mid Atlantic Air Museum in Reading, Pennsylvania, to represent *BRIEFING TIME*.

29

B-25C 41-12566/ *LEGAL EAGLE* **of 1Lt George Bauer, 489th BS/340th BG, Landing Ground 99 (El Kabrit), Egypt, 15 December 1942**

The crew of *LEGAL EAGLE* won the squadron's longest aeroplane name contest by originally calling this machine *SUPERDURCHSCHNITTS-GESCHWIDIDIGKEITER*, which means speedy in German! The bomber completed its 40th mission on 15 December 1942 when it participated in a bombing mission staged by the 340th BG against Axis troop concentrations near the southern Libyan coast.

30

B-25J-1 43-27752/ *LADY ELAINE* **of Capt Clyde Jensen, 489th BS/340th BG, Rimini, Italy, 21 January 1945**

LADY ELAINE was part of a six-aeroplane box (along with three other similar-sized formations) on 21 January 1945 that dropped six 500-lb bombs apiece on bridges in the Po River Valley. Flak was heavy, but all aeroplanes made it safely back to Rimini.

COLOUR SECTION

1

This North American Aviation photograph shows B-25D-15s painted in both Desert Pink and OD parked on the Inglewood, California, ramp awaiting collection in early 1943 (*via the Author*)

2

The 12th BG was the first B-25 Mitchell-equipped bomb group to fly east from the US, arriving in Egypt in July 1942 and initially being placed under the control of No 3 Wing South African Air Force. Here, some of the 12th BG's new Desert Pink B-25Cs are seen approaching the west coast of Africa (*Alex Adair*)

3

B-25C 41-13207 *OH-7* was assigned to the 445th BS. Already kitted out, its six crewmembers walk towards their bomber at the start of yet another mission from North Africa in January 1943 (*M McCandlish via Bob Haney*)

4

Battle-weary B-25J-1 43-27700 was assigned to the 486th BS at Rimini, in Italy in mid 1944 (*USAF*)

5 & 6

The rear gunner's position of 488th BS B-25J-10 43-36230 is prepared for a combat mission by squadron armourers at Gaudo, in Italy, in the spring of 1944 (*Boeing via Peter M Bowers*)

7

486th BS B-25J-1 43-27784 approaches Alesan airfield, on Corsica in early 1944 (*Boeing via Peter M Bowers*)

8

486th BS B-25J-5 43-27900/*BOTTOMS-UP II*, flown by 1Lt Clarence Morton, approaches the airfield at Gaudo in March 1944. Note the yellow-primered engine fairings and tailplane centre section (*Boeing via Peter M Bowers*)

9

B-25J-25 44-30092 of the 12th BG is seen overflying Italy for the last time in March 1944. Just visible on its wing centre-section, painted in red, is the message *FIN TO BENITO NEXT HIROHITO*. The 12th BG left the MTO to fight the Japanese from bases in India in the early spring of 1944 (*USAF*)

10 & 11

B-25H-10 43-5104 *BONES* of the 82nd BS/12th BG was the 1000th, and last B-25H, produced. To mark the occasion, the aircraft was signed by the numerous North American Aviaition employees that had built it at the company's Inglewood plant. Having seen action in the MTO, *BONES* accompanied the rest of the 12th BG to India in March 1944. Never painted, it remained in frontline service until early April 1945, when the bomber collided with a buzzard on approach to landing, forcing the pilot to make an emergency recovery after first performing a go-around. The bird had ripped through the right side of the windshield, just missing the co-pilot, and splattering flesh and feathers all over the underside of the top turret gunner's station. None of the crew were hurt, but *BONES* never flew again. When it was time to salvage the B-25 after the war, it is reported that the smell within its interior was so bad that the scrapping crew (Indian labourers) refused to carry out the work! (*Early Garrett via Bob Haney and Boeing*)

INDEX

References to illustrations are shown in **bold**. Colour Plates are prefixed 'cp.' and Colour Section plates 'cs.', with page and caption locators in brackets.